SPIRITUAL DIRECTION

SPIRITUAL DIRECTION

Wisdom for the Long Walk of Faith

HENRI J. M. NOUWEN
WITH MICHAEL J. CHRISTENSEN
AND REBECCA J. LAIRD

HarperOne
A Division of HarperCollinsPublishers

HarperOne

SPIRITUAL DIRECTION: *Wisdom for the Long Walk of Faith.*
Copyright © 2006 by the Estate of Henri J. M. Nouwen, Michael J. Christensen,
and Rebecca J. Laird. All rights reserved. Printed in the United States of America.
No part of this book may be used or reproduced in any manner whatsoever
without written permission except in the case of brief quotations embodied
in critical articles and reviews. For information address
HarperCollins Publishers, 10 East 53rd Street, New York, NY 10022.

HarperCollins books may be purchased for educational, business,
or sales promotional use. For information please write:
Special Markets Department, HarperCollins Publishers,
10 East 53rd Street, New York, NY 10022.

HarperCollins Web site: http://www.harpercollins.com
HarperCollins®, 📖 ®, and HarperOne™
are trademarks of HarperCollins Publishers.

Library of Congress Cataloging-in-Publication Data
Nouwen, Henri J. M.
Spiritual direction : wisdom for the long walk of faith / Henri J. M. Nouwen
with Michael J. Christensen and Rebecca J. Laird.
p. cm.
Includes bibliographical references.
ISBN: 978-0-06-075473-0
ISBN-10: 0-06-075473-7
1. Spiritual life—Christianity. I. Christensen, Michael J. II. Laird, Rebecca J. III. Title.
BV4501.3.N677 2006
253.5'3—dc22 2006041064

09 10 11 RRD(H) 20 19 18 17 16 15 14 13 12

CONTENTS

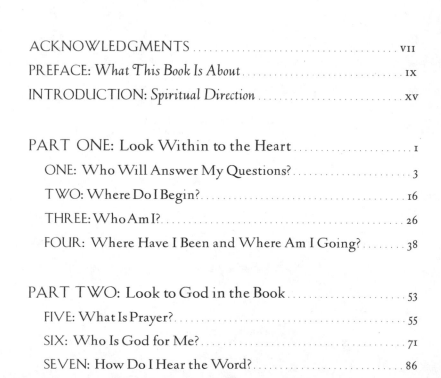

ACKNOWLEDGMENTS

Technically, Henri Nouwen did not write this book, yet the words and wisdom are his. In his lifetime, he wrote only one article with the words *Spiritual Direction* in the title, and he taught only a few courses on "spiritual direction." The book in your hands is a posthumous book of spiritual direction by Henri Nouwen himself, developed by the editors as we identified strands of timeless wisdom and personal guidance in his many sermons, articles, journal records, class lecture notes, unpublished manuscripts, and published writings, and adapted the core material for practical use. The two-year process required the permission and collaboration of the Henri Nouwen Literary Trust to recontextualize Henri, update his language, focus his wisdom, and in many places construct transitions in ways that we trust are true to his meaning and style.

The editors gratefully acknowledge and thank all those who assisted us in producing this book: Steve Hanselman and John Loudon at Harper-Collins, for conceptualizing the project with Rebecca; Sue Mosteller, literary executrix of the Nouwen estate, and the members of the group working on Henri Nouwen Legacy projects—Nathan Ball, Robert Ellsberg, Gabrielle Earnshaw, and Joe Vostermans—for reviewing multiple drafts and guiding us from their knowledge of Henri's life and work; Gabrielle Earnshaw again, in her role as archivist of the Henri J. M. Nouwen Archives and Research Collection, for helping us locate, copy, and verify original source material and the earliest published versions of Henri's writings; John and Carol Lang and Jeff Wittung, Drew University doctoral students, for scanning scores of Nouwen documents for us to weave into the final manuscript; members of the Henri Nouwen Society, especially Jeff Imbach and Virginia Hall Birch, who reviewed the manuscript and offered helpful suggestions; and Mickey Maudlin, Roger Freet, Kris Ashley, and Carolyn Holland, our persistent editorial team at HarperCollins.

Most of all, we thank our teenage daughters, Rachel and Megan, for putting up with our preoccupation with finishing the book before the tenth anniversary of Henri's death, our gift to and labor of love for him. We trust the gift of wisdom and friendship he gave us in life will continue shaping others' lives for years to come.

PREFACE
What This Book Is About

WHEN HE was a young priest, Henri Nouwen understood spiritual direction as a formal relationship for supervision and accountability between a mature spiritual leader and a new priest or minister.[1] Later in life he preferred the term *spiritual friendship,* or *soul friend,* which conveyed the necessary give-and-take in the process of spiritual accountability and faith formation.[2] For Henri, a spiritual director simply was someone who talks to you and prays with you about your life. Wisdom and direction emerge from the spiritual dialogue and relationship of two or more persons of faith committed to spiritual disciplines and the accountability required to live a spiritual life. Thus, spiritual direction as Henri understood it can be defined as *a relationship initiated by a spiritual seeker who finds a mature person of faith willing to pray and respond with wisdom and understanding to his or her questions about how to live spiritually in a world of ambiguity and distraction.*

The spiritual life rests on a paradox, says Henri: "Without solitude, it is virtually impossible to live the spiritual life."[3] Yet we cannot live our spiritual lives alone. Although we need solitude to know God, we require a faithful community to hold us accountable. We need to learn how to listen to the word of God, ever present within our hearts. We need disciplines of study and spiritual practice to discern the word of God in words of scripture. We need a church or faith community that provides opportunities for worshiping and sharing, engaging in mutual correction and bearing of burdens, confessing faults, offering forgiveness, and celebrating life. We also need guides: spiritual friends, a spiritual director, or a spiritual accountability group that can function for us as a safe place to bear our souls.

Henri created community wherever he went, and within those communities he offered spiritual direction, sometimes formally, but mostly in informal conversations and friendships. He also was a spiritual director to many through his personal correspondence, public teachings, and published writings. Before his death, he told his friends that when he died his spirit would be accessible to those he loved and who loved him. Therefore, we trust that your own experience of spiritual direction with Henri Nouwen is possible here and now by the power of the written word and the work of the Holy Spirit.

How This Book Came to Be Written

The idea for this book came out of a simple encounter. During a banquet at which Rebecca was to speak on Henri Nouwen, a young Protestant woman studying to be a spiritual director was seated at her table and told her of some recent struggles. Depression resulting from infertility had rendered her lethargic and despondent. She said, "Reading Henri's books was the only thing that got me through last summer. Through his books, he served as a personal guide through my dark night."

How was it that a male Roman Catholic priest who was in his sixties when he wrote his last books and who never experienced the ups and downs of infertility or marriage was able to touch the wounded heart of this woman? Sure, depression crosses gender and ages, but it was more than that. Henri spoke to universal spiritual needs and longings and understood that what is most personal is also what is most universal. He lived from the depth of the Christian spiritual tradition and knew how to listen for the fundamental questions underlying common human struggles.

Many people turn to Henri's books for spiritual guidance. Yet many of us wish we could have sat knee to knee with Henri and asked our most pressing spiritual questions. But that can no longer be. Henri is physically gone now. We began to wish for a book that would walk readers through the big questions that many people face when they intentionally begin to explore universal spiritual questions and go looking for a guide.

Michael, who benefited from Henri's spiritual guidance in seminary, recalled that he still had his notes from a class Henri taught on spiritual direction at Yale Divinity School. That was enough to get us started. We searched the Henri Nouwen Archives, held at St. Michael's College in Toronto, for his unpublished writings on spiritual formation through spiritual direction. What we found was limited, but wonderful, and required considerable literary knitting and patching.

We pieced together previously unpublished reflections, presentations, homilies, course lecture notes, and recommended exercises. We also wove in material originally published as journal articles, which we found to be more informal and direct than the more polished versions found in his books. We occasionally used excerpts from Henri's books when no better original source was available to cover the subject at hand. The resulting tapestry is our attempt, in collaboration with the Henri Nouwen Literary Trust, to present Henri's approach to some of the big questions of the spiritual life that are often explored in any spiritual direction relationship. Our intention is to provide an experience of doing spiritual direction with Henri Nouwen mediated through his writings and recommended exercises. The edited manuscript, we believe, represents "vintage Henri"—his latest and most mature thinking and relational presence in the practice of offering and receiving spiritual direction. It must be acknowledged, however, that the companionship and accountability that are part of the spiritual direction relationship cannot be replicated or replaced by words on a page. This book, which is intended for both spiritual directors and those seeking direction, is meant to encourage personal reflection and engagement with others as you encounter Henri's wisdom and theological reflection.

We trust that you will find this book to be a tool best used in tandem with holy conversation.

How This Book Can Be Read

The book is designed to be read at least twice: the first time quickly and straight through, perhaps in one sitting; the second time slowly and meditatively, perhaps one chapter a week for ten weeks. You can read the chapters in solitude or in community, in sequence or out of sequence, depending on your questions, needs, and interests. We hope that the "reflect and journal" questions at the end of each chapter are helpful as you reflect and prepare for conversation with others. The exercises at the end of each chapter (most of them used and recommended by Henri) are intended to be done with your spiritual director, soul friend, or small group.

The book is structured around ten universal questions for living the spiritual life. The questions are wrapped in parables, personal narratives, and biblical reflections—which is how Henri structured his spiritual direction and formation classes and retreats. He told short and poignant parables, posed fundamental and perennial questions, selected and reflected on mostly gospel texts, identified countless spiritual disciplines and imperatives, and recommended specific ways to deepen faith.

However read or used, the book is offered as a literary encounter with Henri over a period of time for personal spiritual growth within your own community. Source material is identified at the end of each chapter to leave a paper trail to original texts and contexts. The appendices contain additional resources for recognizing and finding a spiritual director and continuing the discipline of spiritual direction.

We ourselves benefited from Henri's personal spiritual guidance during his lifetime. We've learned from others who knew him best that Henri had a special genius for honing in on spiritual realities and truths in everyday conversation. He had a great gift of friendship and hospitality.

Now that Henri is gone, his wisdom remains. We can still connect with his spirit through the written form. In his physical absence, we all must rely even more on the real guide and director in the spiritual life, who is, of course, the Holy Spirit. Henri, we believe, would approve of this reminder and point us, as he did during his lifetime, continually toward God, the giver, maker, and sculptor of our lives.

Michael J. Christensen
Rebecca J. Laird
January 24, 2006

INTRODUCTION

Spiritual Direction

As WE begin this journey together in spiritual direction,[2] I want to invite you to create space for God in your life. This takes time and commitment. Any spiritual direction commitment affords the opportunity for spiritual friendship, and provides the time and structure, wisdom and discipline, to create sacred space in your life in which God can act. By creating sacred space, you reserve a part of yourself and prevent your life from completely being filled up, occupied, or preoccupied. Spiritual direction provides an "address" on the house of your life so that you can be "addressed" by God in prayer. When this happens, your life begins to be transformed in ways you hadn't planned or counted on, for God works in wonderful and surprising ways.

The goal of spiritual direction is spiritual formation—the ever-increasing capacity to live a spiritual life from the heart. A spiritual life cannot be formed without discipline, practice, and accountability. There are many spiritual disciplines. Almost anything that regularly asks us to slow down and order our time, desires, and thoughts to counteract selfishness, impulsiveness, or hurried fogginess of mind can be a spiritual discipline.

For me, at least three classic disciplines or spiritual practices are particularly useful in the spiritual direction relationship. They can help create space for God within us: (1) the discipline of the Heart, (2) the discipline of the Book, and (3) the discipline of the Church or community of faith. Together, these spiritual practices help us overcome our resistances to contemplative listening and active obedience to God and free us to live an embodied and fulfilled spiritual life.[4]

LOOK WITHIN TO THE HEART

The first and most essential spiritual practice that any spiritual director must ask anyone to pursue is the discipline of the Heart.[5] Introspection and contemplative prayer is the ancient discipline by which we begin to see God in our heart. Interior prayer is a careful attentiveness to the One who dwells in the center of our being. Through prayer we awaken ourselves to God within us. With practice, we allow God to enter into our heartbeat and our breathing, into our thoughts and emotions, into our hearing, seeing, touching, and tasting, and into every membrane of our body. It is by being awake to God in us that we can increasingly see God in the world around us.

The discipline of the Heart makes us aware that praying is not only listening *to* but listening *with* the heart. Prayer helps us stand in the presence of God with all we have and are: our fears and anxieties; our guilt and shame; our sexual fantasies; our greed and anger; our joys, successes, aspirations, and hopes; our reflections, dreams, and mental wandering; and most of all our family, friends, and enemies—in short, all that makes us who we are. With all this we have to listen to God's voice and allow God to speak to us in every corner of our being.

Every corner of our being, of course, includes the physical body. In fact, the "heart" is not purely a spiritual organ but that secret place within us where our spirit, soul, and body come together in a unity of the self. There is no such thing as a disembodied spiritual heart. We are called to love God and neighbor with our whole heart, soul, mind, and strength (Luke 10:27).

This is very hard to do since we are so fearful and insecure. We keep hiding ourselves from God and from others. We tend to present to God and to others only those parts of ourselves with which we feel relatively comfortable and which we think will evoke a positive response. Thus our prayer life becomes very selective and narrow. It is clear that the discipline of the Heart calls for some direction to allow us to overcome fears, to deepen our faith and realize more of who God is for us. Typical questions for a spiritual director to ask are: How is your prayer life? How are you making space in your life for God to speak?

LOOK TO GOD IN THE BOOK

A second discipline held essential in spiritual direction is the discipline of the Book, in which we look to God through *lectio divina*—the sacred reading of the scriptures and other spiritual writings.[6]

When we are really committed to living the spiritual life, we have to listen in a very personal and intimate way to the word of God as it comes to us through the scriptures. The discipline of the Book is the discipline of devotional reading and meditation on a sacred text that leads to prayer. Meditation means to let the word descend from our minds into our hearts and thus to become *enfleshed*. Meditation means eating the word, digesting it, and incorporating it concretely into our lives. Meditation is the discipline by which we let the word of God become a word for us and anchor itself in the center of our being, as well as the wellspring of our actions. In this way, meditation is the ongoing Incarnation of God in our world. The discipline of the Book leads us on the road to true inner obedience. Through the regular practice of scriptural meditation, we develop an inner ear that allows us to recognize God's word that speaks directly to our most intimate needs and aspirations. When we listen to a sentence, a story, or a parable not simply to be instructed, informed, or inspired but to be formed into a truly obedient person, then the Book offers trustworthy spiritual insight. The daily practice of *lectio divina* (sacred reading), over time, transforms our personal identity, our actions, and our common life of faith. A mature spiritual director helps keep our engagement with God's word honest and regular and adds the perspective of communal interpretation. Scripture does have a personal word for us, yet knowledge of historic Christian teaching helps us avoid the easy trap of wanting scripture to support our own designs.

Look to Others in Community

The third discipline key to spiritual direction is the discipline of the Church or faith community. This spiritual practice requires us to be in relationship to the people of God, witnessing to the active presence of God in history and in community "wherever two or three are gathered in my Name" (Matthew 18:20).

A faith community reminds us continuously of what really is happening in the world and in our lives. The church liturgy and lectionary—commonly used prayers, rituals, scripture passages, and a calendar that follows Christ's life throughout the year—unfold for us, for example, the fullness of the Christ-event. Christ is coming, Christ is being born, Christ manifests himself to the world, Christ is suffering, Christ is dying, Christ is being raised up, Christ is ascending into heaven, Christ is sending the Spirit. These events are not simply events that took place long ago and which are remembered with a certain melancholy, but they are events that take place in the day-to-day life of the Christian community. In and through the life of Christ, remembered in community and worship, God makes his active presence known to us. That is what Advent, Christmas, Epiphany, Lent, Easter, Ascension, and Pentecost are all about. The Church calls our attention to the divine events that underlie all of history and which allow us to make sense out of our own story.

To listen to the Church is to listen to the Lord of the Church. Specifically, this means taking part in the Church's liturgical life. During the seasons of Advent, Christmas, Lent, Easter, Ascension, and Pentecost, there are feasts, celebrations, and themes that teach us to know Jesus better and unite us more intimately with the divine life within the community of faith. The more we let the events of Christ's life inform and form us, the more we will be able to connect our own daily stories with the great story of God's presence in our lives. Thus, the discipline of the Church, as a community of faith, functions as our spiritual director by directing our hearts and minds to the One who makes our lives truly eventful. Meeting with a spiritual director provides an interpersonal experience of Christian community and allows for focused conversations on how our individual lives are a part of God's great, unfolding story of God's people.

These three disciplines—the Heart, the Book, and the Church— call for spiritual discernment, accountability, and direction in order to overcome our deafness and resistance, and to become free and obedient persons who hear God's voice even when it calls us to unknown places.

So, if you are interested in starting on the journey, I have a lot more to say to you, because the journey of the spiritual life calls not only for determination and discipline but also for an experiential knowledge of the terrain to be crossed. I don't want you to have to wander about in the desert for forty years, as did our spiritual forebears. I don't even want you to dwell there as long as I did. Although it remains true that everyone has to learn for him- or herself, I still believe that we can caution those we love from making the same mistakes we did. In the terrain of the spiritual life, we need guides. I would like to be your guide. I hope you are interested in walking along.

Henri J. M. Nouwen

PART ONE

Look Within to the Heart

ONE
Who Will Answer My Questions?

A BUDDHIST monk once came to visit me and told me the following story:

~The Zen Master~

Many years ago, there was a young man who searched for truth, happiness, joy, and the right way of living. After many years of traveling, many diverse experiences, and many hardships, he realized that he had not found any answers for his questions and that he needed a teacher. One day he heard about a famous Zen Master. Immediately he went to him, threw himself at his feet, and said: "Please, Master, be my teacher."

The Master listened to him, accepted his request, and made him his personal secretary. Wherever the Master went, his new secretary went with him. But although the Master spoke to many people who came to him for advice and counsel, he never spoke to his secretary. After three years, the young man was so disappointed and frustrated that he no longer could restrain himself. One day he burst out in anger, saying to his Master: "I have sacrificed everything, given away all I had, and followed you. Why haven't you taught me?" The Master looked at him with great compassion and said: "Don't you understand that I have been teaching you during every moment you have been with me? When you bring me a cup of tea, don't I drink it? When you bow to me, don't I bow to you? When you clean my desk, don't I say: 'Thank you very much'?"

The young man could not grasp what his Master was saying and became very confused. Then suddenly the Master shouted at the top of his voice: "When you see, you see it direct." At that moment the young man received enlightenment.[7]

The distance between a Zen Master in the Far East teaching an eager young student and a Christian spiritual director in the West responding to a spiritual seeker might seem a wide bridge to cross. Still, this story powerfully points to the wisdom we need to *live the questions* of our lives, both alone and in community, as we seek our mission in the world.

The young man in the Zen story has unspoken but urgent questions: *What is truth? How may I find joy and happiness? What is the right way of living?* To his, we might add our own life questions: What am I to do with my life? Whom shall I marry? Where shall I live? What gifts do I have to share? What do I do with my loneliness? Why am I so needy for affection, approval, or power? How can I overcome my fears, my shame, my addictions, and my sense of inadequacy or of failure?

Once, quite a few years ago, I had the opportunity of meeting Mother Teresa of Calcutta. I was struggling with many things at the time and decided to use the occasion to ask Mother Teresa's advice. As soon as we sat down I started explaining all my problems and difficulties—trying to convince her of how complicated it all was! When, after ten minutes of elaborate explanation, I finally became quiet, Mother Teresa looked at me and quietly said: "Well, when you spend one hour a day adoring your Lord and never do anything which you know is wrong . . . you will be fine!"

When she said this, I realized, suddenly, that she had punctured my big balloon of complex self-complaints and pointed me far beyond myself to the place of real healing. Reflecting on this brief but decisive encounter, I realized that I had raised a question from below and that she had given an answer from above. At first, her answer didn't seem to fit my question, but then I began to see that her answer came from God's place and not from the place of my complaints. Most of the time we respond to questions from below with answers from below. The result is often more confusion. Mother Teresa's answer was like a flash of lightning in my darkness.

Seeking spiritual direction, for me, means to ask the big questions, the fundamental questions, the universal ones in the context of a supportive community. Out of asking the right questions and living the questions will come right actions that present themselves in compelling ways. To live the questions and act rightly, guided by God's spirit, requires both discipline and courage: discipline to "ask, seek, knock" until the door opens (see Matthew 7:7–8).

What Questions Are People Asking?

You may not be able to formulate an ultimate life question right now. Sometimes we feel so much fear and anxiety, and identify so closely with our suffering, that our pain masks the questions. Once pain or confusion is framed or articulated by a question, it must be lived rather than answered. The first task of seeking guidance then is to touch your own struggles, doubts, and insecurities—in short, to affirm your life as a quest.[8] Your life, my life, is given graciously by God. Our lives are not problems to be solved but journeys to be taken with Jesus as our friend and finest guide.

This is where the ministry of spiritual direction—along with the other interpersonal disciplines of the spiritual life: preaching, teaching, counseling, and pastoral care—can help. These interpersonal resources are intended to help people find a friendly distance from their own lives so that what they are experiencing can be brought into the light in the form of a question to be lived.

A person of faith from long ago who asked and lived the difficult questions of existence was Job. A careful reading of the biblical Book of Job shows that Job's questions are "answered" by his friends, but not by God. As he lives his own questions in the face of suffering, all Job can say is, "The Lord gives and the Lord has taken away; may the name of the Lord be praised" (Job 1:21).

Job's Questions

Job is a good man who loses everything—possessions, land, and family. In the midst of his misery, Job cries out: "Cursed be the day I was born and the night I was thrust from the womb . . . why couldn't I have died as they pulled me out of the womb? Why were there arms to hold me and breasts to keep me alive? If only I had been strangled or drowned on my way to the light!" (Job 3).

And what do his friends—Eliphaz, Bildad, and Zophar—say? They cannot endure his questions and shout at him, "How long will you go on talking, filling our ears with trash?" And bypassing his cry, they start to defend God and themselves. But Job says: "I am sick of your consolations. How long will you fling these words at me? I too could say such things if you were in my place. I could bury you with accusations and sneer at you in my piety." Job receives no help from his friends. By denying his painful questions, they in fact drive him into deeper despair.

When God speaks to Job in the whirlwind, he says: "Were you there when I stopped the waters, as they issued gushing from the womb? When I wrapped the ocean in clouds and swaddled the sea in shadows? Have you seen the gates of death or stood at the gates of doom?" (Job 38). When God sounds through, God speaks through a question that reveals the unspeakable mystery of creative, eternal love.

Thus, to receive spiritual help in time of need requires, first of all, not to deny but to affirm the search. Painful questions must be raised, faced, and then lived. This means that we must constantly avoid the temptation of offering or accepting simple answers, to be easy defenders of God, the Church, the tradition, or whatever we feel called to defend. Experience suggests that such glib apologetics animate hostility and anger, and finally a growing alienation from whom or what we are trying to defend. Be careful when life's questions swirl around you in times of pain. Beware of easy answers or guarantees. Seek the companionship of others who will befriend you and listen as you live the questions of your life.

Any spiritual guide who anxiously avoids the painful search and nervously fills the gap created by unanswerable questions should be viewed with caution. When seeking guidance, we are susceptible to a superficial search for easy answers and shallow meaning. Living into a new way of self-understanding and spiritual depth is aided by having a sturdy spiritual companion or soul friend. The best guides are willing to be silent yet present, and are comfortable with unknowing. God's Spirit is ultimately the sole source of spiritual guidance, comfort, and knowing.

The Zen story of the young man in search of answers and the biblical story of Job living his questions make it clear that no truth can be found unless there is a search for meaning, recognition of human vulnerability and limitation, relationships with trusted spiritual friends, and openness to the disclosure of the transcendent mystery of God, before whom all questions cease.

EMBARK ON A QUEST

The young man in the Zen story goes to a teacher because he has a question. In fact, his whole life has become a question so urgent and compelling that he cries out to the Master: "Please, please be my teacher." Teachers can teach only when there are students who want to learn. Spiritual directors can direct only when there are seekers who come with a question. Without a question, an answer is experienced as manipulation or control. Without a struggle, the help offered is considered interference. And without the desire to learn, direction is easily felt as oppression.

Living the questions runs counter to the mainstream of Christian ministry that wants to impart knowledge to understand, skills to control, and power to conquer. In spiritual listening, we encounter a

God who cannot be fully understood, we discover realities that cannot be controlled, and we realize that our hope is hidden not in the possession of power but in the confession of weakness.

The main questions for spiritual direction—Who am I? Where have I come from? And where am I going? What is prayer? Who is God for me? How does God speak to me? Where do I belong? How can I be of service?—are not questions with simple answers but questions that lead us deeper into the unspeakable mystery of existence. What needs affirmation is the validity of the questions. What needs to be said is: "Yes, yes indeed, these are the questions. Don't hesitate to raise them. Don't be afraid to enter them. Don't turn away from living them. Don't worry if you don't have a final answer on the tip of your tongue."

Spiritual guidance affirms the basic quest for meaning. It calls for the creation of space in which the validity of the questions does not depend on the availability of answers but on the questions' capacity to open us to new perspectives and horizons. We must allow all the daily experiences of life—joy, loneliness, fear, anxiety, insecurity, doubt, ignorance, the need for affection, support, understanding, and the long cry for love—to be recognized as an essential part of the spiritual quest.

The quest for meaning can be extremely frustrating and at times even excruciating, precisely because it does not lead to ready answers but to new questions. When we realize that the pain of the human search is a necessary growing pain, we can accept as good the forces of human spiritual development and be grateful for the journey on the long walk of faith.

WITNESS TO HUMAN VULNERABILITY

When the young Zen student complains that his Master has not taught him anything after three years, the Master responds: "Don't you understand that I have been teaching you during every moment you have been with me?" The reply of the Master powerfully expresses the central role of the spiritual guide. After everything has been said and done, what we have to offer is our authentic selves in relationship to others. What matters most, what transforms, is the influence of a humble, vulnerable witness to the truth.

One of the main objectives of spiritual direction is to help people discover that they already have something to give. Therefore, the director needs to be a receiver who says, "I see something in you, and I'd like to receive it from you." In this way, the one who gives discovers his or her talent through the eyes of the one who receives.

Therefore, the essence of spiritual direction is the quality of *witness,* and witness is the proclamation of what "we have heard, seen with our own eyes, what we have watched and touched with our own hands" (1 John 1:1). To be a witness means to lay down your life for your friends, to become a "martyr" in the original sense of the word. To be a witness means to offer your own faith experience and to make your doubts and hopes, failures and successes, loneliness and woundedness, available to others as a context in which they can struggle with their own humanness and quest for meaning. Instead, we often hide behind our many emotional, mental, and spiritual masks. Who really wants to make their struggles available to others as a source of growth and understanding? Who wants to be reminded of their weaknesses and limitations, doubts and uncertainties? Who wants to confess that God cannot be understood, that human experience is not explainable, and that the great questions of life do not lead to answers but only to deeper questions? Who wants to be vulnerable and say with confidence, "I don't know!" To offer or receive spiritual direction calls for the courage to enter into the common search, confront our brokenness, and use this capacity to grow through wisdom and understanding.

Spiritual direction means to listen to the other without fear and to discover the intimate, divine connections within your own stormy life history. It means to help others discover that their questions are human questions, their search is a human search, and their restlessness is part of the restlessness of the human heart—your own included.

To those with serious struggles and burning questions, I want to reach out with compassion and say: "You seek answers to what cannot be fully known. I don't know either, but I will help you search. I offer no solutions, no final answers. I am as weak and limited as you are. But we are not alone. Where there is charity and love, God is there. Together, we form community. Together we continue the spiritual search."

ASK AND LIVE THE QUESTIONS

As the Zen student gropes for the meaning of his Master's words, the Master suddenly shouts at him: "When you see, you see it direct." At that moment the young man receives enlightenment. This leads to the third aspect of *living the questions*, namely: live the questions until God, sometimes like lightning, reveals enough guidance to enable you to live confidently in the present moment.

To live the questions requires that you first look within yourself, trusting that God is present and at work within you. This is a very difficult task, because in our world we are constantly pulled away from our innermost self and encouraged to look for answers outside of ourselves. If you are a lonely person, you have no inner rest to ask, wait, and listen. You crave people in the hope that another will bring you answers. You want them here and now. But by first embracing solitude in God's presence, you can pay attention to your inner, clamoring self before looking to others for community and accountability. This has nothing to do with egocentrism or unhealthy introspection because, in the words of Rainer Maria Rilke's advice to a young poet, "what is going on in your innermost being is worthy of your whole love."[9]

Frequently, we are restlessly looking for answers, going from door to door, from book to book, or from church to church, without having really listened carefully and attentively to the questions within. Again, Rilke writes to the young poet:

> I want to beg you as much as I can . . . to be patient toward all that is unsolved in your heart and to try to love the questions themselves. . . . Do not now seek answers which cannot be given you because you would not be able to live them. And the point is to live everything. *Live the questions now.* Perhaps you will then gradually, without noticing it, live along some distant day into the answer. . . . Take whatever comes with great trust, and if only it comes out of your will, out of some need of your innermost being, take it upon yourself and hate nothing [emphasis added].[10]

When God enters into the center of our lives to unmask our illusion of possessing final solutions and to disarm us with always deeper questions, we will not necessarily have an easier or simpler life, but certainly a life that is honest, courageous, and marked with the ongoing search for truth. Sometimes, in living the questions, answers are found. More often, as our questions and issues are tested and mature in solitude, the questions simply dissolve.

Seeking guidance and direction will not necessarily yield an easy solution or an answer to the inner quest for meaning. Any teacher or director can only be a mirror reflecting a view, or sometimes an arrow pointing beyond itself. Like the Zen Master in the parable, a spiritual director does not create enlightenment but may help awaken the seeker to receive God's light as a gift.

The greatest call of a spiritual director is to open the door to the opportunities for spiritual growth and sometimes to provide a glimpse of the great mysterious light behind the curtain of life and of the Lord who is the source of all knowing and the giver of life. To receive spiritual direction is to recognize that God does not solve our problems or answer all our questions, but leads us closer to the mystery of our existence where all questions cease.

GOING DEEPER:
EXERCISES FOR SPIRITUAL
DIRECTION

Find a safe and comfortable time and place for prayerful reflection.

In silence and solitude, read the first three chapters of the Book of Job slowly. Pause to consider and reflect on the words spoken by Job and his friends, and also on what is not said but deeply felt between the lines. Let your mind descend into your heart, and listen to the word.

List the friends who surround you. Is there a friend who could sit with you as you ponder the particular questions of your life and simply be present? If so, seek to cultivate that friendship. If not, begin to pray for such a soul friend, spiritual guide, or small group.

Write your question in your journal for further reflection and sharing with your spiritual director or prayer group. You may be helped by following these guidelines for journaling.

GUIDELINES FOR JOURNAL-KEEPING

One of the disciplines of the spiritual life is to keep a journal of personal reflections relating to what scriptures you are reading, your practice of prayer, your experience with a spiritual director, your participation in small-group discussions, and what God is doing in your life.

Writing and reflecting in a journal is not meant to be a chore but an activity for the purpose of spiritual growth. Over time, journal-keeping can become a regular discipline for spiritual formation.

Journal-keeping is meant to be part of the process of asking the deeper questions of the spiritual life, a way of recording how you feel about certain observations, presentations, and ideas and proclaiming what you believe in a context of prayer and listening.

Personal journal-keeping is aided by feedback from others. In your search for an authentic spiritual life, I invite you to choose at least two persons to read selected entries from your journal and offer their comments related to spiritual formation.[11]

REFLECT AND JOURNAL:

Identify and name a persistent question at this time in your life.

Reflect on a time in your life when a painful or persistent question was dismissed or answered glibly by others.

What impact did that response have on you?

TWO
Where Do I Begin?

THE TALE often told about Michelangelo forming a statue speaks
of how spiritual formation takes place in the heart:

~The Lion in the Marble~

There was once a sculptor who worked hard with hammer
and chisel on a large block of marble. A little child who was
watching him saw nothing more than large and small pieces
of stone falling away left and right. He had no idea what
was happening. But when the boy returned to the studio a
few weeks later, he saw, to his surprise, a large, powerful lion
sitting in the place where the marble had stood. With great
excitement, the boy ran to the sculptor and said, "Sir, tell me,
how did you know there was a lion in the marble?"[12]

The little boy's question to the sculptor is a very real one, perhaps the
most important question of all. The answer is, "I knew there was a lion

in the marble because before I saw the lion in the marble, I saw him in my own heart. The secret is that it was the lion in my heart that recognized the lion in the marble." The art of sculpture is, first of all, the art of seeing; and discipline is the way to make visible what has been seen.

Spiritual disciplines are the skills and techniques by which we begin to see the image of God in our heart. Spiritual formation is the careful attentiveness to the work of God, our master sculptor, as we submit to the gradual chipping away of all that is not of God, until the inner lion is revealed. Spiritual direction is the interaction between the little child, the master sculptor, and the emerging, beautiful marble lion. Any director is really an onlooker who cheers and marvels as the artistry unfolds.

Prayerful Listening

Living a spiritual life is far from easy. Marble doesn't give way easily, and neither does the human spirit quickly conform to God's design. Being formed in God's likeness involves the struggle to move from *absurd living* to *obedient listening*. The word *absurd* includes the word *sardus*, which means "deaf." Absurd living is a way of life in which we remain deaf to the voice that speaks to us in our silence. The many activities in which we are involved, the many concerns that keep us preoccupied, and the many sounds that surround us make it very hard for us to hear the "sheer silence" through which God's presence is made known (see 1 Kings 19:12). It seems that the noisy, busy world conspires against our hearing that voice and tries to make us absolutely deaf. It therefore is not surprising that we often wonder, in the midst of our very occupied and preoccupied lives, if anything is truly happening.

Our lives may be filled with many events—so many events that we often wonder how we can get them all done. At the same time, we may feel unfulfilled and wonder if being busy but bored, involved yet lonely, is a symptom of the absurd life: the life in which we no longer hear the voice of the One who created us and who calls us to a new life. This absurd life is extremely painful, because it makes us feel as if we are living in exile, cut off from the vital source of our existence.

The obedient life develops our abilities to hear and sense God's presence and activities. The word *obedience* includes the word *audire*, which means "listening." The obedient life is one in which we listen with great attention to God's Spirit within and among us. The great news of God's revelation is not simply that God exists, but also that God is actively present. Our God is a God who cares, heals, guides, directs, challenges, confronts, corrects, and forms us. God is a God who wants to lead us closer to the full realization of our lionhearted humanity, if you will. To be obedient means to be constantly attentive to this active presence and to allow God, who is only love, to be the source as well as the goal of all we think, say, and do.

Active Resistance to Listening

Developing "ears to hear" God takes time. We all have strong resistances to listening. First of all, we find it very hard to create empty spaces in our lives and to give up our occupations and preoccupations, even for a while. We suffer from a fear of the empty space. We are so concerned with being useful, effective, and in control that a useless, ineffective, and uncontrollable moment scares us and drives us right back to the security of having something valuable to do.

But even stronger than our fear of the empty space is our fear of actually hearing the voice of God! We know that our God is a jealous God who knows there is no other cure for our restlessness and deafness but finding our home in God. We know that God's mercy is a severe mercy that does not coddle or spoil but cuts to the heart where truth resides. And although we are unsatisfied and unfulfilled, we are not so sure that we want to go in the direction God might call us to go. We are not sure our self-image is the same as the image God wishes to form in us. Those who have really listened to God's voice have often found themselves being called away from familiar and relatively comfortable places to places they would rather not go. This was true for the Israelites who complained to Moses that the unpleasant certainty of Egypt seemed preferable to the unpredictable wandering in the desert, and this was true for the many men and women who followed Christ and found themselves subject to persecution and painful trials.

Resistance in the form of preoccupation and distraction often prevents us from seeing the truth of our lives, hearing God's voice, and living a spiritual life. To listen with obedience to the voice of God requires building up a resistance to all the other voices that compete for our attention.

GROWING ATTENTIVENESS

Growing in faith requires a growing attentiveness to perceive where God is active and to where we are being led. One of the key questions in overcoming spiritual deafness and blindness is: Where is God active in my life or community right now?

There is a real tendency to think of the spiritual life as a life that will begin when we have certain feelings, think certain thoughts, or gain certain insights. The problem, however, is not how to make the spiritual life happen, but to see where it actually is happening. We work on the premise that God acts in this world and in the lives of individuals and communities. God is doing something right now. The chipping away and sculpting is taking place whether we are aware of it or not. Our task is to recognize that, indeed, it is God who is acting, and we are involved already in the spiritual life.

A spiritual life doesn't necessarily lead to tranquillity, to peace, or to a beautiful feeling about ourselves or about how nice it is to be together with others. The chipping-away process can hurt. It might mean being lonely in a place where you never wanted to go. It might lead you to a vocation you never sought. It might ask you to do uncomfortable things. Or it might ask you to obediently and routinely do comfortable things that are not very dramatic when you prefer adventure. The spiritual truth is that God is at work in each of us and in our communities and families. Often, the companionship of trusted friends allows us to see how God is at work. We can't always see God's activity by ourselves.

Once this reality is accepted, we are free to say: "Yes, God is speaking to me, God is speaking to us." Then, if we recognize God's claim on us, slowly our eyes are opened, and we begin to see what already has happened. We begin to see the greatness of God revealing itself in daily events, and our lives become a form of obedience. Obedience means, therefore, slowly allowing God's Spirit to draw us to places some of which we might rather avoid. As Jesus said to Peter, "When you were young, you walked where you liked, but when you grow old somebody else will take you where you would rather not go" (John 21:18). Yes, God is a demanding God, God's love is a persistent love, and when God demands a lot from us, it is out of divine love.

DISCIPLINE AND DIRECTION

Because it is so difficult to listen to God's call and obey, we need help in the form of disciplines and practices. Discipline in the spiritual life focuses on the practical side of spiritual formation and is the active companion of belief. Belief, giving your heart over to God's existence and activity, precedes spiritual practice and formation, but belief will be deepened and strengthened by regular spiritual practices.

A spiritual discipline or practice is a way of creating some open and free space in which God can move and speak. For example, the discipline of solitude helps us spend time with God alone and so become aware of the divine silence. The discipline of community helps us to let God speak to us through others. Both solitude and community are disciplines of prayer because in both we try to listen to God. All the disciplines of the spiritual life are intended to help us to move from an absurd (deaf) life to an obedient (listening) life of freedom, joy, and peace.

THE ROLE OF A SPIRITUAL DIRECTOR

A block of marble cannot carve itself, it needs a sculptor. An athlete needs a personal trainer or coach. Likewise, a person of faith will certainly benefit from a spiritual director. We are all very susceptible to self-deception and are not always able to detect our own fearful games or blind spots. How do we know that we are not deluding ourselves, that we are not selecting words of scripture that best fit our passions, or that we are not just listening to the voice of our own imagination? Who can judge their own heart? Who can determine if their feelings and insights are leading them in the right direction? It is too easy to make our heart's desires and our mind's speculations into the will of God.

We need someone who helps us to distinguish between the voice of God and all the other voices coming from our own confusion or from dark powers far beyond our control. We need someone who encourages us when we are tempted to give it all up, to forget it all, and to just walk away in despair. We need someone who cautions us when we move too rashly in unclear directions or hurry proudly toward a nebulous goal. We need someone who can suggest to us when to read and when to be silent, which words to reflect upon, and what to do when silence creates much fear and little peace.

Through the discipline of spiritual direction, we explore in the presence of another wise Christian companion or two God's claim upon our lives, what has been and what may now be. We recognize God's activity and again say yes to the direction in which the Spirit calls us. The direction might be fearful or even quite radical, but we might also be surprised to see that the call of God is a call that is very attractive and that we are able to respond to it because we are being drawn by a loving force.

A spiritual director is someone you ask to hold you accountable for exercising the disciplines and practices of the spiritual life. Spiritual direction, the ancient practice and provision for receiving such needed help, offers prayerful presence, wise counsel, and careful guidance by a spiritual friend who is sensitive to the movements of the Spirit and familiar with the disciplines of the traditions.

FRIENDSHIP, NOT COUNSELING

A spiritual director in this strict sense is not a counselor, a therapist, or an analyst, but a mature fellow Christian to whom we choose to be accountable for living our spiritual life and from whom we can expect prayerful support in our constant struggle to discern God's activity. A spiritual director can be called a "soul friend" or a "spiritual friend" whom we trust to offer wisdom and guidance. The way we relate to our spiritual director depends very much on our present need, our unique personality, and external circumstances. Some people may want to see a spiritual director biweekly or monthly; others will find it sufficient to be in touch only when the occasion asks for it. It is essential that one Christian help another to enter without fear into the presence of God and there to discern God's call.

Spiritual direction and therapy or psychological counseling often appear to be one and the same thing. We are very familiar with words such as *conscious* and *unconscious, depression* and *regression, frustration* and *defense mechanisms, dysfunction, addiction,* and *co-dependency.* Psychological terminology is used more frequently in our society than spiritual words such as *atonement, resurrection, sin, forgiveness,* and *grace.* However, if you simply remain in the psychological world, if you raise only psychological questions, you will get only psychological answers, when your heart needs spiritual wisdom.

WHERE DO I TURN?

During a period of history in which many traditional structures and ways of living are breaking down and we are thrown back on our own personal resources and insights, the need for spiritual direction is increasingly apparent. How then can spiritual direction be offered and received today? Ideally, everyone would benefit from having a personal spiritual director. It would be a mistake, however, to think exclusively about individual spiritual directors. It is important that we start to think about a ministry in which we help one another to practice spiritual disciplines and thus live in such a way that we become more sensitive to the ongoing presence of God in our lives. What finally counts is not just that there are good spiritual men and women in this very chaotic world, but that there are communities of Christians who together listen with great care and sensitivity to the One who wants to make this healing presence known to all people.

Many people today are asking religious leaders, communities of faith, and wise friends to help them find their way through the complex labyrinth of contemporary living. They are asking: How can I become aware of God's presence in my life? How can I have some assurance that my decisions about money, work, and relationships are made in a spiritual way? How do I know that my life is lived in obedience to God and not just in response to my own impulses and desires? For some people, these questions become very specific: Should I live a simpler life? Should I change my ways of eating and dressing? Should I take a more prophetic stand on issues such as war and poverty? Should I give a few years of my life to work with the poor? Such questions seek companionship and discipline in that they require the ability to listen to God's voice. They reflect the areas of our lives where God is at work sculpting our hearts in surprising ways.

GOING DEEPER:
EXERCISES FOR SPIRITUAL
DIRECTION

People who desire a deep and authentic spiritual life often ask for some help. Therefore, it is of great value to submit our prayer life from time to time to the supervision of a spiritual director, counselor, or guide. We are seeking spiritual direction when we are asking the right questions, and desiring to deepen our spiritual life in God. Some people may feel the need for a regular and extensive sharing with their spiritual director, while others find an occasional meeting to be sufficient. Read Appendix Two, "How to Find a Spiritual Director," in which this and other issues are discussed. Whether or not you currently have a personal spiritual director, you can learn to listen and to share your spiritual life with others.

REFLECT AND JOURNAL:

How do I listen attentively to God? What am I hearing right now?

If you imagine yourself as a beautiful but unformed block of marble, what would God need to chip away to reveal the lion inside you?

What other questions would you like to explore with a spiritual director?

THREE
Who Am I?

THE BASIC question "Who am I?" resurfaces throughout life. An old Talmudic tale sheds light on the true identity and value of each and every human being at the deepest level:

~The Fugitive and the Rabbi~

One day a young fugitive, trying to hide himself from the enemy, entered a small village. The people were kind to him and offered him a place to stay. But when the soldiers who sought the fugitive asked where he was hiding, everyone became very fearful. The soldiers threatened to burn the village and kill every person in it unless the young man was handed over to them before dawn. The people went to the Rabbi and asked him what to do. Torn between handing over the boy to the enemy and having his people killed, the Rabbi withdrew to his room and read his Bible, hoping to find an answer before dawn. In the early morning, his eyes fell on these words: "It is better that one man dies than that the whole people be lost."

Then the Rabbi closed the Bible, called the soldiers, and told them where the boy was hidden. And after the soldiers led the fugitive away to be killed, there was a feast in the village because the Rabbi had saved the lives of the people. But the Rabbi did not celebrate. Overcome with a deep sadness, he remained in his room. That night an angel came to him and asked, "What have you done?" He said: "I handed over the fugitive to the enemy." Then the angel said: "But don't you know that you have handed over the Messiah?" "How could I know?" the Rabbi replied anxiously. Then the angel said: "If, instead of reading your Bible, you had visited this young man just once and looked into his eyes, you would have known."[13]

Are we not challenged in daily life to look deeper into the eyes of the people we encounter—even those who are running away from something—and to see in them the face of God? Perhaps just knowing that they too are beloved children of God will be enough to prevent us from handing them over to the enemy. Are we not also challenged and encouraged to look more deeply at the way God sees us—beloved, accepted, affirmed, and worthy of salvation? Are we, like the fugitive, reflections of the Messiah?

You Are the Beloved of God!

When John was baptizing people in the Jordan River, Jesus came to be baptized too. "And as he was praying, the heavens were opened, and the Holy Spirit descended on him in the form of a dove. And a voice came from heaven: 'You are my Son, whom I love, with you I am well pleased'" (Luke 3:21–22).

As a Christian, I am firmly convinced that the decisive moment of Jesus's public life was his baptism, when he heard the divine affirmation, "You are my Beloved on whom my favor rests." In this core experience, Jesus is reminded in a deep, deep way of who he really is.

There is in each of us an inner voice of Love that says: "You are the Beloved of God!" I want you to claim your Belovedness. You don't have to get caught in searches that lead nowhere. Neither do you have to become the victim of a manipulative world or get trapped in any kind of addiction. You can choose to reach out now for true inner freedom and find it ever more fully.

The Ultimate Affirmation

For many years I had read, reflected on, and taught the gospel words in Luke 3 in the story of Jesus's baptism, but only in my later years have they taken on a meaning far beyond the boundaries of my own religious tradition. God's words "You are my Beloved" reveal the most intimate truth about all human beings, whether they belong to any particular tradition or not. The ultimate spiritual temptation is to doubt this fundamental truth about ourselves and trust in alternative identities.

Sometimes we answer the question "Who am I?" with the response, "I am what I do." When I do good things and have a little success in life, I feel good about myself. But when I fail, I start getting depressed. And as I get older and can't do much, all I can say is, "Look what I did in my life . . . look, look, look, I did something good."

Or we might say, "I am what other people say about me." What people say about you has great power. When people speak well of you, you can walk around quite freely. But when somebody starts saying negative things about you, you might start feeling sad. When someone talks against you, it can cut deep into your heart. Why let what others say about you—good or ill—determine who you are?

You might also say, "I am what I have." For example, I am a Dutch person, with kind parents, a fine education, and good health. But as soon as I lose any of it, if a family member dies, if my health goes, or if I lose my property, then I can slip into inner darkness.

How much of our energy goes into defining ourselves by deciding "I am what I do," "I am what others say about me," or "I am what I have"? When that's the case, life often follows a repetitive up-and-down motion. When people speak well about me, and when I do good things, and when I have a lot, I am quite up and excited. But when I start losing, when I suddenly find out that I can't do some task anymore, when I learn that people talk against me, when I lose my friends, then I slip into the pit.

What I want to say to you is that this whole zigzag approach is wrong. I am not what I do, and you are not what you do, or what others say about you, or what you possess. "You are God's Beloved!" I hope that you can hear these words as spoken to you with all the tenderness and force that love can hold. My only desire is to make these words reverberate in every corner of your being—"You are the Beloved!"

The voice that speaks from above and from within whispers softly or declares loudly: "You are my Beloved son or daughter, on you my favor rests." It certainly is not easy to hear that voice in a world filled with voices that shout: "You are no good; you are ugly; you are worthless; you are despicable; you are nobody unless you can demonstrate the opposite."

These negative voices are so loud and so persistent that it is easy to believe them. That's the trap of self-rejection. It is the trap of being a fugitive hiding from your truest identity.

THE TEMPTATION TO DOUBT WHO YOU TRULY ARE

Jesus's temptations in the desert, described in the Gospel of Luke, are temptations to move him away from that core identity. He was tempted to believe he was someone else: You are the one who can turn stone into bread. You are the one who can jump from the temple. You are the one who can make others bow to your power. Jesus said, "No, no, no. I am the Beloved of God." I think his whole life is a continual claiming of that identity in the midst of everything. There are times in which he is praised, times when he is despised or rejected, but he keeps saying, "Others will leave me alone, but my Father will not leave me alone. I am the beloved son of God. I am the hope found in that identity."

The greatest trap in life is not success, popularity, or power, but self-rejection, doubting who we truly are. Success, popularity, and power can indeed present a great temptation, but their seductive quality comes from the way they are part of the much larger temptation to self-rejection. When we have come to believe in the voices that call us worthless and unlovable, then success, popularity, and power are easily perceived as attractive solutions.

How quickly we give in to this temptation of self-rejection. For example, I remember speaking to thousands of people, and many would say, "That was wonderful, what you said." But if one person stood up to say, "Hey, I thought it was a lot of nonsense," that was the only person I would remember. Whenever I feel criticized, rejected, or left alone, I find myself thinking: "Well, that proves once again that I'm a nobody." Instead of taking a critical look at the circumstances or trying to understand my own and others' limitations, I tend to blame myself—not just for what I did, but for who I am. My self-rejection says: "I am no good; I deserve to be pushed aside, forgotten, rejected, and abandoned."

Can you somehow identify in yourself the temptation to self-rejection, whether it manifests itself in arrogance or in low self-esteem? Self-rejection can show itself in a lack of confidence or a surplus of pride. Neither is a true reflection of the core of who we are. Often, self-rejection is simply seen as the neurotic expression of an insecure person. But neurosis is often the psychic manifestation of a much deeper human darkness: the darkness of not feeling truly welcome in human existence. Self-rejection is the greatest enemy of the spiritual life because it contradicts the sacred voice that declares we are loved. Being the Beloved expresses the core truth of our existence. We are loved as creatures with both limitations and glory.

I am putting this so directly and so simply because, though the experience of being the Beloved has never been completely absent from my life, I was slow in claiming it as my core truth. I kept running around it while looking for someone or something able to convince me of my Belovedness. It was as if I kept refusing to hear the voice that speaks from the very depth of my being and says: "You are my Beloved, on you my favor rests."

That soft, gentle voice that calls me the Beloved has come to me in countless ways. My parents, friends, teachers, students, and the many strangers who crossed my path have all sounded that voice in different tones. I have been cared for by many people with much tenderness and gentleness. I have been taught and instructed with much patience and perseverance. I have been encouraged to keep going when I was ready to give up, and was convinced to try again when I failed.

THE TEMPTATION OF COMPULSIVENESS

Coupled with the temptation of doubting who you truly are, is the temptation of compulsiveness. Aren't you, like me, hoping that some person, thing, or event will come along to give you that final feeling of inner well-being you desire? Don't you often hope: "May this book, idea, course, trip, job, country, or relationship fulfill my deepest desire." But as long as you are waiting for that mysterious moment, you will go on running helter-skelter, always anxious and restless, always lustful and angry, never fully satisfied. You know that this is the compulsiveness that keeps us going and busy but at the same time makes us wonder whether we are getting anywhere in the long run. This is the way to spiritual exhaustion and burnout. This is the way to spiritual death.

Well, you and I don't have to dissipate and divide ourselves. We are the Beloved. We were intimately loved long before our parents, teachers, spouses, children, and friends loved or wounded us. That's the truth of our lives. That's the truth I want you to claim for yourself. That's the truth spoken by the voice that says, "You are my Beloved."

Listening to that voice with great inner attentiveness, I hear at my center words that say: "I have called you by name, from the very beginning. You are mine and I am yours. You are my Beloved, on you my favor rests. I have molded you in the depths of the earth and knitted you together in your mother's womb. I have carved you in the palms of my hands and hidden you in the shadow of my embrace. I look at you with infinite tenderness and care for you with a care more intimate than that of a mother for her child. I have counted every hair on your head and guided you at every step. Wherever you go, I go with you, and wherever you rest, I keep watch. I will give you food that will satisfy all your hunger and drink that will quench all your thirst. I will not hide my face from you. You know me as your own as I know you as my own. You belong to me. I am your father, your mother, your brother, your sister, your lover, and your spouse. Yes, even your child. Wherever you are I will be. Nothing will ever separate us. We are one."

THE INVITATION TO RETURN

Dear friend, being the Beloved is the origin and the fulfillment of the life of the Spirit. I say this because, as soon as we catch a glimpse of this truth, we are put on a journey in search of the fullness of that truth and we will not rest until we can rest in that truth. From the moment we claim the truth of being the Beloved, we are faced with the call to become who we are. Becoming the Beloved is the great spiritual journey we have to make. Augustine's words, "My soul is restless until it rests in you, O God," capture well this journey. That I am always searching for God, always struggling to discover the fullness of Love, and always yearning for the complete truth, tells me that I have already been given a taste of God, of Love, and of Truth. I can only look for something that I have, to some degree, already found.

All of us have deep inner memories of the paradise that we have lost. Maybe the word *innocence* is better than the word *paradise*. We were innocent before we started feeling guilty; we were in the light before we entered into the darkness; we were at home before we started to search for a home. Deep in the recesses of our minds and hearts lies the hidden treasure that we once had and now seek. We know its preciousness, and we know that it holds the gift we most desire: a spiritual life stronger than physical death.

If it is true that we not only are the Beloved but also must become the Beloved, how then can we get a grip on this process of becoming? *Becoming the Beloved means letting the truth of our Belovedness become enfleshed in everything we think, say, or do.* It entails a long and painful process of appropriation or, better, incarnation. And this process requires the regular practice of prayer.

THE DISCIPLINE OF PRAYER

Every time you listen with great attentiveness to the voice that calls you the Beloved, you will discover within yourself a desire to hear that voice longer and more deeply. It is like discovering a well in the desert. Once you have touched fertile ground, you want to dig deeper. This digging and searching for an underground stream is the discipline of prayer.

I have come to define prayer as listening to that voice—to the one who calls you the Beloved. The discipline of prayer is to constantly go back to the truth of who we are and claim it for ourselves. My life is rooted in my spiritual identity. We must go back to our first love, back regularly to that place of core identity.

I've said it often that prayer is listening with obedience—listening with careful attention. Jesus listens with obedience to the Father; he keeps listening to the Father's affirmation. Prayer doesn't mean that you have loving, tender feelings as you listen to God's voice.

Sometimes you do, and sometimes you don't. Prayer is a discipline. Discipline means to create boundaries around our meeting with God. Our times and places can't be so filled up that there is no way of meeting. So you have to work very hard to say, this is the time in which I am with God, whether I like it or not, whether I feel like it, whether it satisfies me. You go back to the place of solitude with God and claim who you are.

If I am the Beloved of God, how do I claim my Belovedness? I begin by daily repeating the very words Jesus heard at his baptism, for they are also meant for me and for you: "You are my Beloved. With you I am well pleased." Spend a few minutes every day in prayer, meditating on God's great love.

GOING DEEPER:
EXERCISES FOR SPIRITUAL
DIRECTION

Receive the ultimate affirmation by praying The Beloved Prayer—
a three-part guided meditation composed by Arthur LeClair
for use in solitude, with a spiritual director, or in small prayer
groups.[14]

Sit relaxed and at ease. Have confidence that God's love will
show itself in some way. For the first ten minutes, without fuss,
say the following words slowly and fervently:
Jesus, You are the Beloved.
Repeat the words as necessary. Let your heart fill with nonver-
bal praise and thanksgiving. Let distractions float by, even when
they press upon you. After a while the distractions will seem less
and less urgent as you let them go. Simply be with Jesus in this
precious moment.
Then, gently and without fanfare, move on to the next ten
minutes. Paul reminds us in Romans 9:25 that we too are destined
to become the Beloved. Another color is added to the beauty of
this scene:
Jesus, I am the Beloved.
Let your core-being soak up God's favor. At first, this shift
might seem jarring. But rest in the depth of prayer and let this
truth settle in.
Then go on to the next ten minutes. I used to imagine that
this part would be a distraction, but I have found it to be a rich
and holy connection with others.
Jesus, we (all) are the Beloved.

Let people come into your heart: a neighbor, a friend, a relative, someone you read about in the morning paper. The important thing is not to exclude anyone. Your heart will bring to the surface the ones you need to give attention to.

At the end, simply conclude with a word of thanksgiving, or the Lord's Prayer.

This form of prayer can be done individually or in a group. It can be done on the way to work, in the quiet of early morning, or in the evening before retiring. When you do this as a group, you will find that the members of the group come out of the depths slowly and need a space of silence before speaking again.

Those who have used this prayer speak about a deep healing that takes place within them. If you stay with this form of prayer on a regular basis over a period of time, you will live with a clearer understanding of your place in the universe.

REFLECT AND JOURNAL:

Write a two-sentence answer to the question: Who am I?
What does your answer reveal about what you value?

In what areas of your life are you most prone to self-rejection?

FOUR
Where Have I Been and
Where Am I Going?

WHEN I taught academic courses on the spiritual life, I sometimes drew a long straight line from the left edge to the right on the blackboard, and I'd explain: "This is our eternal life in God. You belong to God from eternity to eternity. You were loved by God before you were born; you will be loved by God long after you die." Then I would mark off a small segment of the line and say: "This is your human lifetime. It is only a part of your total life in God. You are here for just a short time—for twenty, forty, sixty, or eighty years—to discover and believe that you are a beloved child of God. The length of time doesn't matter. Life is just a short opportunity for you during a few years to say to God: 'I love you, too.'"

As a parable of this truth, I want to tell you the true story of my friend from L'Arche named Adam.[15] I want to tell it from a divine perspective, as if God were the storyteller. God has a story of Adam *from above* that only God can fully tell, a story for us to try to hear:

~God's Story of Adam~

Long, very long, before I gave Adam to his parents, long before he was born among his fellow human beings, I knew him and loved him. He belonged to me as my beloved child. I carried him from all eternity in my heart and mind and cared for him as for the apple of my eye. Then one day I sent him to the planet earth to live among people. Because he would be a man invited to suffer, I entrusted him to a loving woman and a caring man who were to be his parents. I sent him to be a silent witness who would bring my message of love through his great vulnerability. I know that few people are capable of fully accepting a gift hidden in brokenness. Therefore, I chose with great care these two people so that they could help me in revealing that gift to the world.

For thirty-four years Adam lived among his brothers and sisters. He was not able to speak, walk without assistance, go regularly to school, find a job, earn a living, or have a wife and children. He didn't give talks, write books, or win a prize. He simply was present among people as a silent witness to my love.

Then, on February 13, 1996, I saw that Adam had fulfilled his mission and I called him back home to me. I gave him a voice so he could tell me all he had experienced on the earth and in a body that would allow him to walk, run, and dance in my presence to everyone's delight. I am so glad to have him back, and I know for sure that having been where he was, he will give special attention to all who loved him and cared for him but also to all the people whose brokenness he shared.[16]

Are you ready to hear this story from above? Doesn't this story echo the story of Jesus, God's own beloved child? Isn't this your story and mine? Can you imagine God smiling when we discover the secret that Adam's story, your story, my story, and the story of Jesus are in truth one and the same story? We all have been loved by God before and beyond time. As the Lord said through the prophet Jeremiah: "I have loved you with an everlasting love" (Jeremiah 31:3). And as the Psalmist declares: "You created me in my inmost being; you knit me together in my mother's womb" (Psalm 139:13). Sometimes it takes a lifetime to see, hear, and believe God's story of us.

Two Voices

From the beginning of my life, two interior voices have been speaking to me: one saying, *Henri, be sure you make it on your own. Be sure you become an independent person. Be sure I can be proud of you;* and another voice saying, *Henri, whatever you are going to do, even if you don't do anything very interesting in the eyes of the world, be sure you stay close to the heart of Jesus, be sure you stay close to the love of God.*

I'm sure we all hear these voices to some degree—one that says, *Make something of your life, find a good career,* and one that says, *Be sure you never lose touch with your source and vocation.* There's a struggle, a tension, here.

At first, I tried to resolve this by becoming a sort of hyphenated priest—a priest-psychologist. People would say, "We don't really like having priests around," and I could reply, "Oh well, I'm a psychologist. I'm clearly in touch with sophisticated things, so don't laugh at me or disregard me."

Early in life I pleased my father and mother immensely by studying, then teaching, and then becoming somewhat well known, teaching at Notre Dame, Yale, and Harvard Universities. I pleased a lot of people doing so and also pleased myself. But somewhere on the way up the ladder I wondered if I was still in touch with my core identity and vocation. I began noticing this when I found myself speaking to thousands of people about humility and at the same time wondering what they were thinking of me.

I didn't feel peaceful. Actually, I felt lost. I didn't know where I belonged. I was pretty good on the platform but not always that good in my own heart. I began to wonder if, perhaps, my career hadn't gotten in the way of my vocation. So I began to pray: "Lord Jesus, you know me and love me with an everlasting love. Let me know where you want me to go, and I will follow you. But please be clear about it. No ambiguous messages!" I prayed this over and over.

One morning at nine o'clock someone pushed the bell of my little apartment. I opened the door and found a young woman standing there.

"Are you Henri Nouwen?"

"Yes, I am."

"I've come to bring you the greetings of Jean Vanier," she continued.

Jean Vanier was all but unknown to me at the time. I'd heard he was the founder of the L'Arche communities and that he worked with mentally handicapped people, but that was all I knew.

I said, "Oh, that's nice. Thank you. What can I do for you?"

"No, no, no," she answered. "I've come to bring you the greetings of Jean Vanier."

Again I said, "Thank you, that's nice. Do you want me to talk somewhere or write something or give a lecture?"

"No, no," she insisted. "I just wanted you to know that Jean Vanier sends his greetings."

When she had gone, I sat in my chair and thought, *Now, this is something special. Somehow is God answering my prayer, bringing a message and calling me to something new?* I wasn't asked to take a new job or do another project. I wasn't asked to be useful to anybody. I simply was invited to come to know another human being who had a message for me.

Three years later, I finally met Jean Vanier at a silent retreat during which no words were spoken. At the end, Jean said, "Henri, maybe L'Arche can offer you a home, a place where you are really safe, where you can meet God in a whole new way." He didn't ask me to be useful; he didn't ask me to work for handicapped people; he didn't say he needed another priest. He simply said, "Maybe we can offer you a home."

Gradually I realized I had to take that call seriously. I left Harvard University and went to the L'Arche community at Trosly-Breuil in France. After spending a year with this community of mentally handicapped people and their assistants who try to live in the spirit of the Beatitudes, I responded to the call to live as a priest at Daybreak, which is a L'Arche community near Toronto, a community of about 150 handicapped people and 50 assistants.

This is how I tell my story, but God also has a story of me, a story I must try to hear. My teacher in the school of sacred history—God's story of me—was Adam, one of the 150 members of that community.

My Life with Adam

The first thing asked of me when I arrived at L'Arche was to help Adam with his morning routine. (Of all names, Adam! It sounded like working with humanity itself.) Adam, a twenty-four-year-old, was not able to talk, nor was he able to walk. Adam was not able to dress or undress himself. Even though he followed me with his eyes, it was difficult to know for sure whether or not he actually knew me. He was limited by a body that was misshapen, and he suffered from frequent epileptic seizures.

At first with Adam I was afraid, and so working with him was not easy for me. I would rather have been teaching at the university because I knew how to do that! I had no experience of caring so intimately for another human being. "Don't worry," the other assistants assured me. "Soon you will really meet Adam, and then you will know how to hold him, how to be with him."

I went to his room at seven in the morning. I gently woke him and helped him get up. I held him up and very carefully walked with him to the bathroom because I was frightened that he might have a seizure. When I had undressed him, I struggled to help him into the bathtub, as he was as heavy as I am. I started to pour water over him, wash him, shampoo his hair, and take him out again to brush his teeth, comb his hair, and return him to his bed. Then I dressed him and held him from behind as we walked together to the kitchen.

When he was safely seated at the table, I offered him breakfast. He was able to lift the spoon to his mouth. Mainly because Adam loved to eat and enjoyed all his meals to the full, we ate together and I carefully watched him as he ate. It took a while, and I was aware that I had never sat silently watching with anyone, especially a person who took about an hour to eat breakfast.

Then something transpired: after two weeks, I was a little less frightened. After three or four weeks, it dawned on me that I was thinking a lot about Adam and looking forward to being with him. I realized something was happening between us—something intimate and beautiful that was of God. I don't know how to explain it very well.

God was speaking to me in a new way through this broken man. Little by little, I discovered affection in myself and came to believe that Adam and I belonged together. To put it simply, Adam silently spoke to me about God and God's friendship in a concrete way.

First, he taught me that *being* is *more important than doing*, that God wants me to be with him and not do all sorts of things to prove I'm valuable. My life had been doing, doing, doing. I'm a driven person, wanting to do thousands and thousands of things so that I can show—somehow, finally—that I'm worthwhile.

People had said, "Henri, you're okay." But now, here with Adam, I heard, "I don't care what you do, as long as you will be with me." It wasn't easy just to be with Adam. It isn't easy simply to be with a person and not do much.

Adam taught me something else: *the heart is more important than the mind.* When you've come from an academic culture, that's hard to learn. Thinking with the mind, having arguments, discussing, writing, doing—that's what a human being is. Didn't Thomas Aquinas say that human beings are thinking animals? Giving high priority to an intellectual approach to life was a deeply honed value in me.

Well, I'm not certain about how Adam thought, but gradually I became convinced that Adam had a heart, a real human heart. All at once I saw that what makes a human being human is the heart with which one can give and receive love. In giving himself so totally into my hands, Adam was giving me an enormous amount of God's love from a trusting heart, and I was giving Adam of my love. There was an intimacy that went far beyond words or acts.

When the physical, emotional, intellectual, or moral life commands all the attention, we are in danger of forgetting the primacy of the heart. The heart is that divine gift that allows us to trust, not just God, but also our parents, our family, ourselves, and our world. Very small children seem to have a deep, intuitive knowledge of God, knowledge of the heart that sadly is often obscured and suffocated by the many systems of thought we gradually acquire. People with physical and mental disabilities easily can let their hearts speak and thus reveal a mystical life unreachable by many intellectually astute people. This is because the mystical life, the life of the heart, originates in God at the very beginning of our existence. We belong to God from the moment of our conception. We are born in intimate communion with God, who created us in love. And we will die into the loving arms of God, who loves us with an everlasting love.

I am ashamed to say that it took me some time to move from thinking that Adam, far from being primarily physically and mentally challenged and therefore not my equal, was in fact my brother. He was a full human being, so fully human that he was chosen by God to become the instrument of his love. Adam's vulnerability gave space for the heart. Adam, for me, became just heart—the heart in which God chose to dwell, in which he wanted to speak to those who came close to Adam's vulnerable heart.

And I understood too what I had learned in Latin America a few years earlier about God's "preferential option for the poor." Indeed, God loves the poor, and God loved Adam very specially. He wanted to dwell in Adam's broken body so that he could speak from that vulnerability into the world of strength and call people to become vulnerable and to offer their brokenness to God in ministry.

Finally, Adam taught me something about community. *Doing things together is more important than doing things alone.* I came from a world concerned with doing things on one's own, but here was Adam, so weak and vulnerable and dependent on others. And I couldn't help Adam alone. We both needed all sorts of people. At L'Arche Daybreak, we had people from Brazil, the United States, Canada, and Holland—young and old—living together in one house around Adam and other handicapped people. As the weakest link among us, Adam created community. He brought us together; his needs and his vulnerability made us into a true and loving community. With all our differences, we could not have survived as a community if Adam hadn't been there. His weakness became our strength, our rallying point.

That's what I learned from Adam, God's beloved son. I lived at Daybreak ten years before Adam died. His story is my story of weakness, vulnerability, and dependency, but also of strength, authenticity, and giftedness.

Can you dare to believe that God's story about you puts your story in spiritual perspective? One way to do this is to write down your personal story without editing out your vulnerability and brokenness and to be willing to tell your story to others. This is the discipline of witness in the world. Here's how I would tell my sacred story, trusting in the truth of God's story of me.

MY HISTORY WITH GOD

At the core of my faith belongs the conviction that I am a beloved child of God. If I were to draw a line on a flip chart, I would say:

That's my life, my little chronology, my little clock time. I was born in 1932, and I wonder where the end point will be? Maybe 2010, maybe earlier. A few more years are really all I have. Life goes by very, very fast.[17]

My first twenty-four years of life were basically years to prepare myself for the Catholic priesthood. I was born and raised in a Roman Catholic family, went to Roman Catholic schools, and lived a life in which I related exclusively to Roman Catholics. It was a time in which all the boundaries were clear. I was a Roman Catholic and not a Protestant; I was Christian and not Muslim, Buddhist, or Hindu; I was a believer and not a pagan; I was a man and not a woman; I was Dutch and not German, French, or English; I was white and not black, etc. These very clear boundaries gave me a sense of being in the right place, being wholly protected, and being very safe. I never met anybody who was divorced, who had left the priesthood, or who was gay. It was very clear what I was going to do as a priest. I knew the right teaching and the right way to live the moral life. Six years in the seminary had given me very clear-cut guidelines and surrounded me with people who had received the same guidelines. Proclaiming the Gospel and administering the sacraments were challenging but not complicated, and something I really felt called to do. I was a very happy person, felt very close to God, and had a very disciplined prayer life and a very clear-cut vocation. I was ordained in July 1957.

After my ordination, I studied psychology at the Catholic University of Nijmegen in Holland, visited the Vatican Council, worked as chaplain of the Holland America Line, and was trained as a reserve army chaplain. I then studied for a few years at the Menninger Clinic to explore the relationship between religion and psychiatry, taught for two years at Notre Dame, ten years at Yale, and three years at Harvard, and made visits to Latin America. During all these years

I learned that Protestants belong as much to the Church as Catholics, that Hindus, Buddhists, and Muslims believe as much in God as Christians, that pagans can love one another as much as believers, that the human psyche is multidimensional, that theology, psychology, and sociology are intersecting in many places, that women have a real call to ministry, that homosexual people have a unique vocation in the Christian community, that the poor belong to the heart of the Church, and that the Spirit of God blows where it wants. All of these discoveries gradually broke down many fences that had given me a safe haven and made me deeply aware that God's covenant with God's people includes everyone. For me personally it was a time of searching, questioning, and often agonizing. A time that was extremely lonely and not without moments of great inner uncertainty and ambiguity. The Jesus that I had come to know in my youth had died.

When I joined the L'Arche Daybreak community in Toronto, Canada, in 1986, I was searching for a new home. I knew it could not be the old home that I had left, but I did not know what the new home would look like. During the last few years living with people with mental handicaps and their assistants in a very close-knit community consisting of people from many different religions, backgrounds, communities, and lifestyles, my heart started to burn, and I started to recognize the presence of Jesus in a radical new way. During this time I have experienced much loneliness, much confusion, and much insecurity, but I experienced all of this sorrow living with poor people who in their simplicity and openness offered me a space that gradually could become a new home. Since living in community, my spiritual journey has been radically deepened, the full dimension of which I am not yet fully able to articulate. But I know that living with the people of my community is calling me to be a witness to God in a way that I never could have been before. It is only in retrospect that I can connect the dots on the timeline of life and begin to see my sacred history from God's perspective—as God's story of me.

Now you may draw your life line on the flip chart to the right of mine and say, "I came here." And you may draw your end point a little to the right of mine and say, "I have a few more years to go." And as you begin to tell your story and to connect the dots, it is good to realize that, although life is short, it is enough time to come to understand where you have been and where you are going.

Remember: You belong to God from eternity to eternity. You were loved by God before you were born; you will be loved by God long after you die. Your human lifetime—long or short—is only a part of your total life in God. The length of time doesn't matter. Life is just a little opportunity for you during a few years to say to God: "I love you, too."

GOING DEEPER:
EXERCISES FOR SPIRITUAL DIRECTION

All of us have a history with God, whether or not we are conscious of it. Our history with God affects the way we listen, read, speak, think, and pray. Although our personal story is unique, it is part of a greater story—God's story of our lives. When we claim and share our sacred history, we bear witness to others that God has a greater story about each of us.

I invite you to explore your own spirituality and claim your own story as sacred history as it has emerged during your lifetime. The following questions may be helpful in writing and presenting your sacred history for your small group or spiritual director:

1. What moments in your life with God stand out as crucial in your spiritual journey? Describe these moments succinctly and indicate their main intellectual, emotional, and spiritual significance.

2. When you think of the three major disciplines of the spiritual life (looking within to the heart, looking to God in the Book, and looking to each other in community), where do you see your greatest gifts and your greatest need?

3. What persons, books, movements, ideas, etc., have played a significant role in your spiritual growth?

In your journal, write a three paragraph reflection on your own sacred history based on one of these three questions. Then, share it with your spiritual director, soul friend, or prayer group.

REFLECT AND JOURNAL:

How has a period of discontent or an encounter with a special person challenged your life or changed your life course?

PART TWO

Look to God in
the Book

FIVE
What Is Prayer?

As we look to God in the heart, we do so in relation to the word of God through prayer. "What is prayer?" "How to pray?" "How often to pray?" are the questions explored in this chapter. Leo Tolstoy crafted a parable that gets to the heart of true prayer:

~Three Monks on an Island~

Three Russian monks lived on a faraway island. Nobody ever went there, but one day their bishop decided to make a pastoral visit. When he arrived, he discovered that the monks didn't even know the Lord's Prayer. So he spent all his time and energy teaching them the "Our Father" and then left, satisfied with his pastoral work. But when his ship had left the island and was back in the open sea, he suddenly noticed the three hermits walking on the water—in fact, they were running after the ship! When they reached it, they cried, "Dear Father, we have forgotten the prayer you taught us."

The bishop, overwhelmed by what he was seeing and hearing, said, "But, dear brothers, how then do you pray?" They answered, "Well, we just say, 'Dear God, there are three of us and there are three of you, have mercy on us!'" The bishop, awestruck by their sanctity and simplicity, said, "Go back to your land and be at peace."[18]

There is a difference between learning *prayers* and *prayerfulness,* as Tolstoy's famous parable illustrates. The prayerfulness of the heart is deeper and ultimately more important than *particular* prayers that are said. Prayers are specific expressions of praise and thanksgiving, confession and petition, supplication and intercession. Examples of particular prayers are the "Lord's Prayer" and the "Jesus Prayer." Prayerfulness, however, is a matter of the heart, mostly unspoken, that reveals itself in gentleness, peacefulness, humbleness, compassion, and other fruit of the Spirit (see Galatians 5:22–23). In Tolstoy's story, it is the monks who pray in spirit and in truth, and the bishop who recognizes their sanctity and prayerfulness, despite their ignorance of the "Our Father."

Daily prayers and a spiritually-cultivated quality of prayerfulness throughout the day make possible the Apostle Paul's admonition to "pray without ceasing."

Unceasing Prayer

To the Christians in Thessalonica, Paul writes: "Always be joyful; pray constantly; and for all things give thanks; this is the will of God in Christ Jesus" (1 Thessalonians 5:17–18). Paul not only encourages unceasing prayer, but also practices it. "We continually thank God for you" (1 Thessalonians 2:13), he says to his community in Greece. "We also pray continually that our God will make you worthy of his call" (2 Thessalonians 1:11). To the Romans, he writes: "I continually mention you in my prayers" (Romans 1:9), and he comforts his friend Timothy with the words: "I remember you in my prayers constantly, night and day" (2 Timothy 1:3).

The two Greek terms that appear repeatedly in Paul's letters are *pantote* and *adialeiptos,* which mean "always" and "without interruption." These words make it clear that for Paul, prayer is not a part of living, but all of life, not a part of his thought, but all of his thought, not a part of his emotions and feelings, but all of them. Paul's fervor allows no place for partial commitments, piecemeal giving, or hesitant generosity. He gives all and asks all.

This radicalism obviously raises some difficult questions. What does it mean to pray without ceasing? How can we live life, with its many demands and obligations, as an uninterrupted prayer? What about the endless row of distractions that intrude day after day? Moreover, how can sleep, needed moments of diversion, and the few hours in which we try to escape from the tensions and conflicts of life be lifted up into unceasing prayer? These questions are real and have puzzled many Christians who want to take seriously Paul's exhortation to pray without ceasing.

One of the best-known examples of the desire for unceasing prayer is the nineteenth-century Russian peasant who wanted so much to be obedient to Paul's call for uninterrupted prayer that he went from *staretz* to *staretz* (hermit to hermit) looking for an answer until he finally found a holy man who taught him the Jesus Prayer. He told the peasant to say thousands of times each day, "Lord Jesus Christ, have mercy on me." In this way, the Jesus Prayer slowly became united with his breathing and heartbeat so that he could travel through Russia carrying his knapsack with the Bible, the *Philokalia* (an anthology of Eastern Christian mystical writings), and some bread and salt, living a life of unceasing prayer.[19]

Although we are not nineteenth-century Russian peasants or pilgrims, we share the quest of the simple pilgrim: "How to pray without ceasing?" I want to answer this question not in the context of the wide, silent Russian prairies of a century ago but in the context of the restlessness of our contemporary Western society. I suggest that the practice of unceasing prayer is a threefold process: we first *cry out to God* with all our needs and requests. Then we turn our unceasing thoughts into continual *conversation with God.* Finally, we learn to listen to God in our hearts through a daily discipline of *meditation and contemplative practice.*

Prayer as Crying Out to God

Prayer, first of all, is crying out to God from our heart. "Give ear to my words, O Lord, and consider my sighing" is a prayer from the heart. "Listen to my cry for help, my King and my God, for to you do I pray" (Psalm 5:1–2).

There is so much fear and agony in us. Fear of people, fear of God, and much raw, undefined, free-floating anxiety. I wonder if fear is not our main obstacle to prayer. When we enter into the presence of God and start to sense that huge reservoir of fear in us, we want to run away into the many distractions that our busy world offers us so abundantly. But we should not be afraid of our fears. We can confront them, give words to them, cry out to God, and lead our fears into the presence of the One who says: "Don't be afraid, it is I."

Our inclination is to reveal to God only what we feel comfortable in sharing. Naturally, we want to love and be loved by God, but we also want to keep a little corner of our inner life for ourselves, where we can hide and think our own secret thoughts, dream our own dreams, and play with our own mental fabrications. We are often tempted to select carefully the thoughts that we bring into our conversation with God.

What makes us so stingy? Maybe we wonder if God can take all that goes on in our minds and hearts. Can God accept our hateful thoughts, our cruel fantasies, and our bizarre dreams? Can God handle our primitive urges, our inflated illusions, and our exotic mental castles? This withholding from God of a large part of our thoughts leads us onto a road that we probably would never consciously want to take. It is the road of spiritual censorship—editing out all the fantasies, worries, resentments, and disturbing thoughts we do not wish to share with anyone, including God, who sees and knows all.

When we hide our shameful thoughts and repress our negative emotions, we can easily spiral down the emotional staircase to hatred and despair. Far better it is to cry out to God like Job, pouring out to God our pain and anger and demanding to be answered.

A number of years back, Pierre Wolff wrote a wonderful little book on *uncensored* prayer. It is called *May I Hate God?* and it touches on the very center of our spiritual struggle. Our many unexpressed fears, doubts, anxieties, and resentments, he says, prevent us from tasting and seeing the goodness of the Lord. Anger and hatred, which separate us from God and others, can also become the doorway to greater intimacy with God. Religious and secular taboos against expressing negative emotions evoke shame and guilt. Only by expressing our anger and resentment directly to God in prayer will we come to know the fullness of love and freedom. Only in pouring out our story of fear, rejection, hatred, and bitterness can we hope to be healed.[20]

The Psalms are filled with the raw and uncensored cries and agonies of God's people, poured out to God and asking for deliverance. For example:

> *My God, my God, why have you forsaken me. . . . I cry out by day, but you do not answer, by night, and am not silent. (Psalm 22:1–2)*

> *I cried out to God for help: I cried out to God to hear me. When I was in distress, I sought the Lord; at night I stretched out untiring hands and my soul refused to be comforted. (Psalm 77:1–2)*

> *Hear, O Lord, and answer me, for I am poor and needy. (Psalm 86:1)* [21]

The more we dare to show our whole trembling self to God, as did the ancients who prayed the Psalms, the more we will be able to sense that God's love, which is perfect love, casts out our fears, purifies our thoughts, and heals our hatred.

Prayer as Conversation

Secondly, when monologue moves to dialogue, prayer becomes simple, intimate conversation with the Lord who loves us. For example, when I pray the psalm "When I call, answer me, O God of justice; from anguish release me, have mercy and heal me!" (Psalm 4:2), sometimes I hear God answer: "I am with you . . ." and all shall be well. Sometimes in the night I pray, "O God, come to my assistance; O Lord, make haste to help me," and hear God answer:

"God is for us a refuge and strength, a helper close at hand, in time of distress." (Psalm 45:1). And when I tell God how lonely and unloved I feel, I often sense God's reassurance: "Strong is his love for us; he is faithful forever" (Psalm 116:2). After I pray, I try to listen to God's voice and to keep the word I hear with me throughout the day. Mediated through the word, prayer becomes spiritual conversation with the One who knows and loves me.

To pray unceasingly, as St. Paul asks us to do, would be completely impossible if it meant to think constantly about or speak continuously to God. To pray unceasingly does not mean to think about God in contrast to thinking about other things, or to talk to God instead of talking to other people. Rather, it means to think, speak, and live in the presence of God. Although it is important and even indispensable for the spiritual life to set apart time for God and God alone, prayer can only become unceasing prayer when all our thoughts—beautiful or ugly, high or low, proud or shameful, sorrowful or joyful—can be thought and expressed in the presence of God. Thus, converting our unceasing thinking into unceasing prayer moves us from a self-centered monologue to a God-centered dialogue. This requires that we turn all our thoughts into conversation. The main question, therefore, is not so much what we think, but to whom we present our thoughts.

It is not hard to see how a real change takes place in our daily life when we find the courage to keep our thoughts to ourselves no longer but to speak them out, confess them, share them, bring them into conversation. As soon as an embarrassing or exhilarating idea is taken out of its isolation and brought into a relationship, with God or with another person, something new happens. Once we take the risk and experience acceptance, our thoughts themselves receive a new quality and are transformed into prayer.

Prayer, therefore, is not introspection. It does not look inward but outward. Introspection easily can entangle us in the labyrinth of inward-looking analysis of our own ideas, feelings, and mental processes and can lead to paralyzing worries, self-absorption, and despair. Prayer is an outward, careful attentiveness to the One who invites us to an unceasing conversation. Prayer is the presentation of all thoughts—reflective thoughts as well as daydreams and nightmares—to our loving Father who can see them and respond to them with divine compassion. Prayer is the joyful affirmation that God knows our minds and hearts without anything being hidden. It is saying with the Psalmist:

> O Lord, you search me and you know me,
> you know my resting and my rising,
> you discern my purpose from afar.
> You mark when I walk or lie down,
> all my ways lie open to you.
> Before ever a word is on my tongue
> you know it, O Lord, through and through. (Psalm 138:1–4) [22]

Prayer as Contemplation

Finally and fundamentally, prayer is an attitude of an open heart, silently in tune with the Spirit of God, revealing itself in gratitude and contemplation. Prayer is not just crying out to God for help (although it certainly starts there), or talking with God about our thoughts; prayer is a silent listening that leads to contemplation in the presence of God. Particular prayers can become *prayerfulness* of the heart through cultivating an attitude of gratitude and a spirit of contemplation.

As we learn how to pray, somewhere along the way we experience the crying out to God about our needs as a monologue, a one-sided affair. And even when prayer becomes a dialogue, with God speaking and answering our prayers, we long for more of God's presence. The truth is that prayer is more than feeling, speaking, thinking, and conversing with God. To pray also means to be quiet and listen, whether or not we feel God is speaking to us. More than anything, prayer is primarily listening and waiting. We listen for God in an attitude of openness of heart, humility of spirit, and quietness of soul. We let our mind descend into our heart and there stand in the presence of God.

One way to stand in the presence of God and pray unceasingly is to meditate by using the Jesus Prayer. In the parable Jesus tells about the Pharisee and the tax collector in Luke 18, the tax collector's simple prayer—"Lord, have mercy on me a sinner"—was heard and became known in the Eastern Orthodox tradition as the Jesus Prayer. Repeating the simple phrase "Lord Jesus, have mercy" very slowly takes on a meditative quality that brings peace and repose to the soul. The words can become part of our breathing, of our whole way of being. The beautiful thing about the Jesus Prayer is that we can take prayer with us in our work—while we drive our car, while we sit behind a desk to study, even while we eat or fall asleep. Thus, we can pray without ceasing.

Over time our particular prayers become prayerfulness, and the quality of prayerfulness makes us more aware of the divine presence. Gradually we learn that God is not a silent God who does not want to be heard or experienced. God is not a resistant God who has to be manipulated into paying attention to us. God is not a reluctant God who has to be convinced to do something good for us. No, we come to realize that God is a God of compassion, "slow to anger and abounding in steadfast love," who came to dwell in our midst, and who longs to be listened to so that healing can come.

To summarize, prayer is a crying out to God, a simple conversation, and a contemplative listening in the presence of God who loves us. Once we learn these aspects, we can make prayerfulness a daily practice and thus, as the Apostle Paul says, "pray without ceasing" (1 Thessalonians 5:17).

THE DISCIPLINE OF PRAYER

Prayer is not something that comes naturally or easily. It is something that requires learning and discipline. This is true both for saying particular prayers and for remaining in a continuing attitude of prayerfulness. In learning to pray, it is important to set aside a *definite time*, a *special place*, and a *single focus*.

A Definite Time

Our time for prayer could be in the morning, at noonday, or at night. It could be an hour, a half-hour, or ten minutes. It could be once or more times each day. The important thing is to commit to a definite time during the day to be alone with God in prayer.

The question is not "Should I pray?" but "When will I pray?" Before you go to work? During a break in the middle of the day? At night before you fall asleep? Most people find that early in the morning is the best time of the day to set aside for prayer, as Jesus did (see Mark 1:35). If that is unrealistic, then set aside some other time during the day when God will get your full attention. Any half-hour or so during the day is better than no time at all. Without a half-hour of prayer in the morning or at night, or ten minutes of prayer during the day, or a brief prayer before dinner or after dinner, we begin to forget that God is near and that our life in God is a life of prayer.

A Special Place

Once we have set aside our time for God, we are free to follow Jesus's words: "Go to your private room, shut the door, and so pray to your Father who is in that secret place" (Matthew 6:6). Not only time but place is important in prayer. Choose a special place to pray the Psalms, meditate on the word, or contemplate the glory of the Lord. Jesus often chose to climb a mountain, enter a garden, depart to the desert, or rest in a boat on the water to pray and listen to God. The Apostle Paul, when in the city of Philippi, looked for a special place of prayer along a river bank (Acts 16:13). Outdoors or inside, wherever you are most comfortable, find a quiet and peaceful spot for prayer and meditation.

The ideal is to have a special room in your home to set aside for prayer. If such a room is decorated with images that speak about God, when there are some candles to light or perhaps some incense to burn, then you will more often want to be there. And the more you pray in such a place, the more that place will be filled with the energy and power of prayer. In such a place, it won't be hard to leave the world behind for a moment and to let yourself be absorbed by the love of Jesus.

In case you don't have a room to spare, find a "prayer closet" or a corner of a room to set up an altar or claim a special chair for prayer. And if that is not possible, try to go to a church or chapel where you feel safe and where you want to return. While it is true that you can pray anywhere, a particular time and special place designated for regular solitary prayer is best.

A Single Focus

What do you do during the time and place for prayer? The simple answer is: just be with Jesus. Let him look at you, touch you, and speak to you. Believe that you are in God's presence. Speak in any way your heart desires. And learn to listen. Let God be the single focus of your time set apart to be in the presence of the Lord.

For most of us, this simple answer is not enough. The complication is that as soon as we enter into solitude, we discover how tired or bored we are. Of course, if we are physically exhausted, we cannot pray. The most spiritual thing we can do then is to take a nap. When we are bored, the time feels empty and useless.

But why not spend some "useless" time in our busy days in prayer? Prayer is not being *busy with* God, as opposed to being busy with someone or something else. Prayer is primarily a "useless" hour to be with God, not because I am so useless to God, but because I am not in control. If anything useful comes out of my prayer, it is God who does it. Over time, our time spent with God may become more fruitful. But this is not of our doing. The time set apart for prayer is in our control, but the results are not.

Once we are alert and ready for prayer, the thing to do is to find a focus. Read the gospel text for the day, sing a psalm, or pick out a verse of scripture and read it slowly.

In all the great spiritual traditions, those who practice prayer or meditation have a single point of concentration. For Christians, the focus may be the name "Jesus." Or it may be the Jesus Prayer: "Lord have mercy." It may be a compelling image, a powerful word, or a phrase in scripture—something that commands your attention. The purpose of focusing your prayer is to free the mind to meditate with the heart and contemplate the glory of God.

DEALING WITH DISTRACTIONS

When we are learning how to pray with a single focus, we find out how chaotic our inner life has become. Suddenly, all sorts of distracting thoughts, feelings, and fantasies come to the surface. Soon we feel like a banana tree filled with jumping monkeys. Our mind is full of things to do: the letter we have to write, the telephone calls we have to make, a dinner engagement we have to keep, an article we have to write, an insight we have to capture, where we'd rather be, our worries and concerns, etc.

Don't be surprised at this. You can't just suddenly shut the door of a house that was always open to strangers and expect no one to knock at the door again. You do not fight distractions by pushing things away, but by focusing on one thing. It's like looking at a candle for a long time. Slowly you start feeling quiet as you focus on something else, and then the distractions begin to vanish. With practice, you can learn to acknowledge the distractions, choose not to act on them, send them away, and return to your primary purpose, which is prayer.

So when a distraction intrudes into your prayer, smile at it, let it pass, and return to your chosen focus. Repeat the words of the Psalm, read again the gospel lesson, return to the image of contemplation, continue meditating with your chosen word. Eventually, the words you speak with your lips or in your heart, the images you gaze at and see through, the sensations you feel when you pray, will become increasingly attractive to you, and soon you will find them much more important and enjoyable than the many "oughts" and "musts" that try to slip into your spiritual consciousness. Words that come from God have the power to transform your inner life and create there a home where God gladly dwells.

Be Faithful

The important thing is faithfulness in prayer. Stay with it as a discipline of daily life. If you choose a definite time, a special place, and a single focus for prayer, then slowly the boredom lessens, the distractions diminish, and God's presence is found. Once you learn to pray at certain times and places, and with a single focus, you may find that it is possible to remain in an attitude of prayer and gratitude throughout the day. This is what St. Paul means when he says, "Pray without ceasing." This is what Jesus means when he calls prayer "the only necessary thing" (Luke 10:42).

Let me offer a prayer for you as you continue to make prayer a part of your life and trust that God will help one day grant you the knowledge that you have begun to pray without ceasing.

> *Lord Jesus Christ, have mercy on me. Let me know you as my loving brother who holds nothing—not even my worst sins—against me, but who wants to touch me in a gentle embrace. Take away my many fears, suspicions, and doubts by which I prevent you from being my Lord, and give me the courage and freedom to appear naked and vulnerable in the light of your presence, confident in your unfathomable mercy, and willing to listen to you at all times and places. Amen.*

GOING DEEPER:
EXERCISES FOR SPIRITUAL
DIRECTION

THE DISCIPLINE OF PRAYER

I invite you to try following a prayer discipline for ten minutes a day or so for a week, and then to discuss your experience with your spiritual director or prayer group.

1. Simply set apart a specific time and place to "waste" a little time alone with yourself and God. What time of the day will you pray, and where will you pray?
2. Add to your particular time and special place a single focus. This can be an image, a word, a phrase of scripture, or a short meditative prayer that is repeated.
3. When distractions come or you feel anxious or sleepy, acknowledge the distraction—don't fight it—then simply return to your image, phrase, or scripture.
4. Embrace the silence between the repetitions in prayer. This is how you create space for God to be present.
5. Sometimes, within our sacred time and place and focus, God speaks a simple word for us to hear. Learn to listen to the still, small voice.

Many people who do this regularly eventually find that they don't want to miss their prayer time—even though it doesn't emotionally satisfy them right away. They may be distracted throughout the whole ten minutes, but they keep going back to it. They say that "something is happening to me on a deeper level than my thinking."

I too don't always have wonderful thoughts or feelings when I pray. But I believe that something is happening because God is greater than my mind and heart. The larger mystery of prayer is greater than what I can grasp with my emotional senses or intellectual gifts. I trust that God is greater than me when I dwell—let myself be held—in that place of prayer. Eventually, when I do this I do live a very spiritual life.

REFLECT AND JOURNAL:

What parts of your life are you tempted to hide from God?

What thoughts are you thinking right now? Stop to offer them to God as a conversational prayer.

What time, place, and focus for prayer will you commit to this week?

SIX
Who Is God for Me?

ONE GOOD way to answer big questions like *Who is God? To whom am I praying?* and *Who is God for me?* is to tell stories such as the old Indian tale about the four blind men and the elephant:

~Four Blind Men and the Elephant~

There are four blind men who discoverer an elephant. Since the men have never encountered an elephant before, they grope about, seeking to understand and describe this new phenomenon. One grasps the trunk and concludes it is a snake. Another explores one of the elephant's legs and describes it as a tree. A third finds the elephant's tail and announces that it is a rope. And the fourth blind man, after discovering the elephant's side, concludes that it is, after all, a wall.

Which one is right? Each in his blindness is describing the same thing: an elephant. Thus, all are right, but none wholly so.[23]

Who Is the One to Whom I Pray?

When I was staying at Genesee Abbey, I asked the Abbot a very basic question: "When I pray, to whom do I pray?" or, "When I say 'Lord,' what do I mean?"

The Abbot responded very differently than I expected. He said, "Indeed, this is the real question, this is the most important question you can raise." He stressed with great convincing emphasis that if I really wanted to take that question seriously, I should realize that there would be little room left for other things. Knowledge of God is a subject one can never fully master.

"It is far from easy," he said, "to make that question the center of your meditation. You will discover that it involves every part of yourself because the question 'Who is the God to whom I pray?' leads directly to the question 'Who am I who wants to pray to God?' And then you will soon wonder about God's multivalent character, and ask, 'Why is the God of justice also the Lord of love; the God of fear also the God of gentle compassion?' This leads you to the center of your heart—the core of our being." What the Abbot meant by "heart" includes the deep recesses of our psyche, our moods and feelings, our emotions and passions, also our intuitions, insights, and visions. The heart is the place where we are most human. A listening heart therefore means a heart in which we stand open to God with all of our questions, with all that we are, and with all that we have. That is a great act of trust and confidence.

"In the quiet meditation of the listening heart, is there an answer?" I asked. "Yes and no," said the Abbot. "You will find out in your meditation. You might someday have a flash of understanding even while the question still remains and pulls you closer to God.

But it is not a question that can be simply *one* of your questions. In a way, it needs to be your only question around which all that you do finds its place. It requires a certain decision to make that question the center of your meditation."

BE STILL AND KNOW

Psalm 46 speaks to us about how to make the question of God the center of our life and how to find the God who wants to be found:

> *God is our refuge and strength, an ever-present help in trouble.*
> *Therefore we will not fear, though the earth gives way and the*
> *mountains fall into the heart of the sea, though its waters roar*
> *and foam and the mountains quake with their surging. There is*
> *a river whose streams make glad the city of God, the holy place*
> *where the Most High dwells. . . . "Be still and know that I am God.*
> *I will be exalted among the nations, I will be exalted in earth."*
> *(Psalm 46:1–4, 10)*

The Psalmist similarly hears God declare: *"Be still and know that I am God.* Be still and know what kind of God I am. Be still and know that I am who I am and that I will be there for you."

Each of the four blind men in the parable touch a part of the elephant, just as four persons of faith are in touch with different aspects of God. All know the truth about the reality they touch, but none wholly so. Reflecting on the wisdom of this story in relation to the question of God in the Psalm, I wish to say four things about God, realizing that though these things may be true, none are fully so. First, *God is with us*. Second, *God is personal*. Third, *God is hidden*.

And fourth, *God is looking for us.* Then I want to challenge you to "be still and know" in your heart that God is God.

GOD IS WITH US

Truly the good news is that God is not a distant God, a God to be feared and avoided, a God of revenge, but a God who is moved by our pains and participates in the fullness of the human struggle. God is a compassionate God. This means, first of all, that God is a God who has chosen to be with us. As soon as we call God, "God-with-us," we enter into a new relationship of intimacy. By calling God *Immanuel,* we recognize that God is committed to live in solidarity with us, to share our joys and pains, to defend and protect us, and to suffer all of life with us. God-with-us is a close God, a God whom we call our refuge, our stronghold, our wisdom, and, even more intimately, our helper, our shepherd, our love. We will never really know God as a compassionate God if we do not understand with our heart and mind that God came and lived among us and with us (John 1:14).

The way God is with us is through the word made flesh in Jesus, who walks beside us with love and understanding. I remember a critical time when the Lord walked with me in a special way. After being hit by the mirror of a passing van, I ended up in the hospital with five broken ribs and a bleeding spleen. My life was in real danger. As I faced surgery, I let myself enter into the portal of death. What I experienced was pure and unconditional love. I heard a Voice say: "Don't be afraid. I am with you." When the nurses strapped me on the operating table, I let go of my fear and felt an immense inner peace. I was told I had lost two-thirds of my blood and had narrowly escaped death. Although Jesus was there to greet me, I was sent back for a purpose—to speak the truth from Above to below, from Eternity into time. Emmanuel—*God is with us.*

GOD IS PERSONAL

A second truth about God is that God is with us in a personal way. I traveled to St. Petersburg in July 1986 to study Rembrandt's painting of *The Return of the Prodigal Son.* While sitting in front of the painting in the Hermitage, trying to absorb what I saw, many groups of tourists passed by. Even though they spent less than a minute with the painting, almost all of the guides described it as a painting of the compassionate father. Instead of being called *The Return of the Prodigal Son,* it could easily have been called *The Welcome by the Compassionate Father.*

Looking at the way Rembrandt portrays the father, there came to me a whole new interior understanding of tenderness, mercy, and forgiveness. Seldom, if ever, has God's immense, compassionate love been expressed in such a poignant and human way. The most divine qualities are captured in the most human gestures and relationships. God, the creator of heaven and earth, has chosen to be, first and foremost, a loving parent expressed most often in the New Testament as *Abba,* a kind, gentle, and most intimate father.

Abba is a very intimate word. The best translation for it is "Daddy." The word *Abba* expresses trust, safety, confidence, belonging, and, most of all, intimacy. It does not have the connotations of authority, power, and control that the word *father* often evokes. On the contrary, *Abba* implies an embracing and nurturing love that comes to us from our fathers, mothers, brothers, sisters, spouses, friends, and lovers.

Calling God "Abba, Father" is different from giving God a familiar name. Calling God "Abba" is entering into the same intimate, fearless, trusting, and empowering relationship with God that Jesus had. This relationship is called Spirit, and this Spirit is given to us by Jesus and enables us to cry out with him, "Abba, Father."

Calling God "Abba, Father" is a cry of the heart, a prayer welling up from our innermost being (see Romans 8:15 and Galatians 4:6). It has nothing to do with labeling God but everything to do with claiming God as the source of who we are. This claim does not come from any sudden insight or acquired conviction; it is the claim that the Spirit of Jesus makes in communion with our spirits. It is the claim of love.

A closer look at Rembrandt's painting also reveals the image of a loving mother receiving her son home. God is personal yet beyond gender and limitations. What I see in Rembrandt's painting in the welcoming figure is not only a father who "clasps his son in his arms" but also a mother who caresses her child, surrounds him with the warmth of her body, and holds him against the womb from which he sprang. Every time I look at the tent-like and wings-like cloak in Rembrandt's painting, I sense the motherly quality of God's love, and my heart begins to sing in the words inspired by the Psalmist:

> *[You] who dwell in the shelter of the Most High*
> *and abide in the shade of the Almighty—say to your God:*
> *My refuge, my stronghold, my God in whom I trust!*
>
> *. . . You conceal me with your pinions*
> *and under your wings, I shall find refuge. (Psalm 90)* [24]

The deeper meaning of the "return of the prodigal son" is the return to God's womb, the return to the very origins of being, and again echoes Jesus's exhortation to Nicodemus to be reborn from above.

What I see here is God as Mother, receiving back into her womb the one whom she made in her own image. The near-blind eyes, the hands, the cloak, the bent-over body, they all call forth the divine maternal love, marked by grief, desire, hope, and endless waiting.

The mystery, indeed, is that God in her infinite compassion has linked herself for eternity with the life of her children. She has freely chosen to become dependent on her creatures, whom she has gifted with freedom. This choice causes her grief when they leave; this choice brings her gladness when they return. But her joy will not be complete until all who have received life from her have returned home and gathered together around the table prepared for them.

The parable of the prodigal son is a story that speaks about a love that existed before any rejection was possible and that will still be there after all rejections have taken place. It is the first and everlasting love of a God who is Father as well as Mother.

GOD IS HIDDEN

A third aspect of God is a very difficult one to accept: God is hidden as well as able to be found, absent as well as present. The hidden and mysterious aspect of God is celebrated in the classical mystical text *The Cloud of Unknowing*.[25]

When we first experience the reality of God's presence in our lives, when we return home to God's personal and loving embrace, we are initially sheltered from the truth of the hiddenness and absence of God. Eventually, we may come to understand that this too is an aspect of divinity.

Ultimately, we discover that God cannot be understood or grasped by the human mind. The full truth of God escapes our human capacities. The only way to come close to it is by a constant emphasis on human limits to "have" or "hold" the whole truth. We cannot explain God or God's presence in history. As soon as we identify God with any specific event or situation, we play God and distort the truth. We can be faithful only in our affirmation that God has not deserted us but calls us in the middle of all the unexplainable absurdities of life.

As you consciously seek to be formed by God, it is very important to be deeply aware of this. There is a great temptation to suggest to myself or others where God is working and where not, when God is present and when not, but nobody, no Christian leader, priest, or pastor, no monk or nun, and no spiritual director has any "special" knowledge about God. The fullness of God cannot be limited by any human concept or prediction. God is greater than our mind and heart and perfectly free to be revealed where and when God wants.

Dietrich Bonhoeffer in *Letters and Papers from Prison* writes: "The God who is with us is the God who forsakes us (Mark 15:34). Before God and with God we live without God."[26] In meditating on the question "Who is God and who is God for me?" we touch the terrifying truth that our fragile lives in fact vibrate between two sides of the darkness. We hesitantly come forth out of the darkness of birth and slowly vanish into the darkness of death. We move from dust to dust, from unknown to unknown, from mystery to mystery.

We try to keep a vital balance on the thin rope of life that is stretched between the two definitive poles that mark our chronological lives. We are surrounded by the reality of the unseen and the unknown, which fills every part of our life with terror but at the same time holds the secret mystery of our being alive. That secret is this: "though we walk in darkness, we have seen a great light" (Matthew

4:16). And this light, while it can be masked, cannot go out, as it shines for all eternity.

The light of God is *beyond* the darkness—beyond our hearts and minds, beyond our feelings and thoughts, beyond our expectations and desires, and beyond all the events and experiences that make up our lives. Still God is in the center of all of it.

In prayer and mediation, God's presence is never separated from God's absence, and God's absence is never separated from God's presence in the heart. The presence of God is so much beyond the human experience of being near to another that it quite easily is misperceived as absence. The absence of God, on the other hand, is often so deeply felt that it leads to a new sense of God's presence. This is powerfully expressed in Psalm 22:1–5:

> *My God, my God, why have you forsaken me?*
> *The words of my groaning do nothing to save me.*
> *My God, I call by day but you do not answer,*
> *at night, but I find no respite.*
> *Yet you, the Holy One,*
> *who make your home in the praises of Israel,*
> *in you our ancestors put their trust,*
> *they trusted and you set them free.*
> *To you they called for help and were delivered;*
> *in you they trusted and were not put to shame.*

This prayer of abandonment is not only the expression of the experience of the people of Israel but also a centerpiece of the Christian experience. When Jesus echoed these words on the Cross, total aloneness and full acceptance touched each other. In that moment of complete emptiness, all was fulfilled. In that hour of darkness, new light was seen. While death was witnessed, life was affirmed. Where God's absence was most loudly expressed, God's presence was most profoundly revealed.

The mystery of God's presence therefore can be touched only by a deep awareness of God's absence. It is in our longing for the absent God that we discover the footprints of the Divine One. It is in the realization of God's presence that we know that we have been touched by loving hands. It is *into* this mystery of divine darkness and divine light—God's absence and God's presence—that we enter when we pray.

Once we enter into the center of our heart, or what the mystics call the "cloud of unknowing," we come to know God in a deeper way as our creator, redeemer, and sustainer, as the God who is the source, the center, and the purpose of our existence, as the God who wants to give us unconditional, unlimited, and unrestrained love, and as the God who wants to be loved by us with all our heart, all our soul, and all our mind.

In the cloud of unknowing, the distinction between God's presence and God's absence dissolves. It is the place of the great encounter, from which all other encounters derive their meaning. It is the place where the various glimpses of God—God-with-us, God as Father and Mother, God as absent yet present—come together as one. In the solitude of the heart, in the depths of the soul, in the cloud of unknowing, we meet God.

God Is Looking for Us

A fourth truth about the God to whom we pray is that God is seeking us. We do not find God, but God finds us.

God is the good shepherd who goes looking for the lost sheep. God is the woman who lights a lamp, sweeps out the house, and searches everywhere for her lost coin until she has found it. God is not the patriarch who stays home, doesn't move, and expects his children to come to him, apologize for their sinful behavior, beg for forgiveness, and promise to do better. God is the father who watches and waits for his children, runs out to meet them, embraces them, pleads with them, and begs and urges them to come home. It might sound strange, but God wants to find us as much, if not more, than we want to find God.

For most of my life I have struggled to find God, to know God, to love God. I have tried hard to follow the guidelines of the spiritual life—pray always, work for others, read the scriptures—and to avoid the many temptations to dissipate myself. I have failed many times but always tried again, even when I was close to despair.

Now I wonder whether I have sufficiently realized that during all this time God has been trying to find me, to know me, and to love me. The question is not "How am I to find God?" but "How am I to let myself be found by God?" The question is not "How am I to know God?" but "How am I to let myself be known by God?" The question is not "How am I to love God?" but "How am I to let myself be loved by God?" And finally, the question is not "Who is God for me?" but "Who am I to God?"

The good news is that God is scanning the horizon for me, trying to find me, and longing to bring me home. In the same way, God is looking for you.

GOING DEEPER:
EXERCISES FOR SPIRITUAL
DIRECTION

How would you answer the eternal questions of the heart: *Who is God? What is God like? Who is God for me?* Discuss this with your spiritual director or prayer group.

Reflect on Psalm 46 and discuss in a small group the four "partial truths" about God's nature and desire: God is with us, God is personal, God is hidden as light beyond the darkness and as presence in the absence, and God is looking for us where we are. Which truth relates most to your spiritual experience? Discuss this with your spiritual director or prayer group.

I want to challenge you to develop a discipline of contemplative prayer and meditation—a way to "be still and know" in your heart that God is looking for you. Imagine the prophet Elijah on Mount Horeb. He did not experience the presence of God in the mighty wind, nor in the powerful earthquake, nor in the consuming fire. He heard God speak in a whisper, in a still, small, gentle voice (see 1 Kings 19:9–13). Imagine the community gathered around the camp singing Psalm 46. God had delivered them from the tempest of roaring mountains, falling rocks, and surging waters. God was their refuge and strength, an ever-present help in trouble. Therefore they did not fear. Instead, they sang and became still. They listened for God's whisper. The practice of contemplative prayer and meditation makes us more sensitive to God's whisper.

In this spirit, as an exercise, I offer you a simple meditation on Psalm 46:10.[27] Read it in solitude, or listen as someone else reads it slowly and interspersed with silence in a small circle of friends. Then discuss your experience of meditation with your spiritual director or soul friend.

A Guided Meditation on Psalm 46:10

Be still and know that I am God.

Be still: Be quiet. . . . Be silent. . . . Be tranquil. Be present. . . . Be now. . . . Be here. . . .

The first task of the disciple is to be with the Lord . . . to sit at His feet, to listen and to be attentive to all He says, does, and asks.

Our Lord is all we need and want. . . . Our stronghold, our refuge, our shepherd, our wisdom. God cares for us, feeds us . . . gives us life . . .

Be still. . . . It is hard. . . . It means to let God speak to us . . . breathe in us . . . act in us . . . pray in us. . . . Let God enter into the most hidden parts of our being . . . let God touch us even there where it may hurt us and cause us pain. . . .

To be still is to trust . . . to surrender . . . to let go . . . to have faith.

Be still. . . . God is and God acts . . . not once in a while . . . not on special occasions . . . but all the time. . . . Be still and listen to the one who speaks to you always, feel the actions of the one who acts always . . . and taste the presence of the one who is present always.

Know: Come to know . . . real knowledge . . . full intimate knowing.

A form of diagnosis . . . a knowing through and through. A knowing with the heart, a knowing by heart. . . . Be still and know. Come to that still knowledge. There is a very restless knowledge, a confusing, distracting, dividing knowledge . . . but knowing God . . . is a knowing of the heart . . . of the whole person. It is a knowing that is also seeing, hearing, touching, smelling.

Be still and know that I am God.

That is not meant to be a fearful knowledge . . . but a peaceful knowledge. God is not a God of the dead, but a God of the living, God is not a revengeful God, but a God of Love. Know that I am God . . . your God. The God who is only love . . . the God who touches you with his limitless and unconditional love.

Be still and know that I love you . . . that I hold you in the palm of my hand . . . that I have counted the hairs of your head . . . that you are the apple of my eye . . . that your name is written in my heart. . . . "Do not be afraid . . . it is I."
There is nothing in us that needs to be hidden from God's love. Our guilt . . . our shame . . . our fear . . . our sins . . . He wants to see it, touch it, heal it . . . and make himself known. There is no other God than the Lord of Love.

Be still and know that I am God. God is not in the storm, nor in the earthquake, nor in fire, but in the still, small voice, the gentle breeze, and the sheer silence . . .

Be still and know that I am God. Take these words with you in the week to come. . .let them be like a little seed planted in the good soil of your heart and let it grow . . .

Be still and know that I am God.

CLOSING PRAYER

O Lord, I know now that it is in silence, in a quiet moment, in a forgotten corner of my heart that you will meet me, call me by name, and speak a word of peace. Let me be still and know you by name.

REFLECT AND JOURNAL:

How do you picture God? What does God look like and sound like when you close your eyes?

When have you felt God's absence? What is the impact of this unwelcome or unfamiliar aspect of God on your faith?

When have you felt God's personal presence? How has this experience strengthened your faith?

SEVEN
How Do I Hear the Word?

HERE ARE three sayings of the Desert Fathers about hearing the word of God. Together they reveal the variant meanings of *word.*

~Word and Wisdom~

In Scetis, a brother went to see Abba Moses and begged him for a word. And the old man said: Go and sit in your cell, and your cell will teach you everything.

A brother asked Abba Hieracus: Give me a word. How can I be saved? The old man said to him: Sit in your cell; if you are hungry, eat; if you are thirsty, drink; and just do not speak evil of anyone, and you will be saved.

Abba Hyperichius, from the silence of his cell, said: The person who teaches others by actions, not by words, is truly wise.[28]

During the fourth and fifth centuries, among the Desert Fathers and Mothers in the Egyptian desert, it was not uncommon for a novice to find an older monk and ask: "Abba, do you have a word for me?" Often, the Abba would help the seeker listen for the *word* of God. These desert Christians seeking to find God in the word meant three things by *word.* First of all, they meant the *Living Word* (*Logos*), which is Jesus. Secondly, they meant the *written word,* which is Holy Scripture. And thirdly, they meant a *spoken word* (*rhema*), which flows forth from a prophet out of silence and humbleness of heart and which speaks to one's current condition. The Living Word, the written word, and a spoken word are three ways God speaks to us. And to these three I want to add a fourth: *writing the word,* thoughtfully and prayerfully, so as to encourage your own participation in hearing and recognizing the word in your own lives.

LISTENING TO THE LIVING WORD OF GOD

Listening to the eternal, creative Living Word, both hidden and revealed in the life and teaching of Jesus, is the first way we encounter Jesus. The Gospel of John begins this way:

> In the beginning was the Word, and the Word was with God. He was with God in the beginning. Through him all things were made; without him nothing was made that has been made. In him was life, and that life was the light of human beings. The light shines in the darkness, but the darkness has not understood it. (John 1:1–5)

This passage from John highlights a core truth about Jesus: he somehow existed before creation, enlivens human beings, and transcends time and all creation. This type of word isn't restricted to a page, it creates and acts. John uses the Greek word *logos* to capture this meaning.

My own words sometimes lose their creative power. In contrast to the many words that define our existence is this creative word of God. The Living Word is born out of the eternal silence of God, and it is to this creative word out of silence that we want to bear witness.

Before the word was incarnated in her womb, Mary bore witness to the word of God. Because of her obedient listening, the word could become flesh in her. Listening is a very vulnerable stance. Mary was so vulnerable, so open, and so receptive that she could listen with her whole being. Nothing in her resisted the word that was announced to her by the angel. She was "all ears" and heart. Thus, the promise could be fulfilled in her far beyond her own understanding and control. "I am the Lord's servant," Mary said. "May it be to me as you have said" (Luke 1:38).

Listening is the core attitude of the person who is open to God's living and creative word. Prayer is listening to God, being open and receptive to God's influence. True listening has become increasingly difficult in churches and institutions, where people remain on their guard, afraid to expose their weaker side, eager to be recognized as successful and bright. In our contemporary competitive society, listening often is a way of "checking the other person out." It is a defensive stance in which we do not really allow anything new to happen to us. It is a suspicious way of receiving that makes us wonder what serves our purposes and what does not. The psalmist warns against this hardening of the heart:

> *Today, listen to the voice of the Lord;*
> *Do not grow stubborn, as your fathers and*
> *mothers did in the wilderness,*

When at Meriba and Massah they challenged
me and provoked me,
Although they had seen all my works. (Psalm 95:7–9)

The word of God here is to listen to the voice of love and not to harden your hearts.

This kind of listening asks us to model our lives on Jesus and to commit to follow the way of life Jesus set forth. This listening assumes a personal prayer life and a belief in Jesus's activity in the world today as the Living Word of God.

Listening to the incarnate word of life is the heart of Christian faith. In Mary, we see the purest form of this listening. That is why she is called "blessed" by her cousin Elizabeth. It is through her obedience to the word that became flesh in her that she becomes not only the mother of God but also the mother of all the faithful. We who wish to be faithful are called to this same kind of obedience. When we listen faithfully to the word, the word becomes flesh in us and dwells among us.

Jesus, the Word of God, is hidden in humanity. In him, God became a human being among a small, oppressed people, under very difficult circumstances. There was nothing spectacular about his life. Even when you look at Jesus's miracles, you find that he did not heal or revive people in order to get publicity. He often forbade them even to talk about it. He was held in contempt by the rulers of his country and was put to a shameful death between two criminals. His resurrection was a hidden event. Only his disciples and a few of the women and men who had known him intimately before his death saw him as the risen Lord. Neither his life nor death nor resurrection was intended to astound us with the great power of God. God became a lowly, hidden, almost invisible God in bodily form. And this is the real power of the word.

Perhaps you think about the word of God as a divine exhortation to go out and change your life. But the full power of the word lies not in how you apply it to your life after you have heard it but in how its transforming power does its divine work in you as you listen.

READING THE WORD

A second way to encounter God is to listen to the living word *in* the written word of God. Reading, meditating, and listening to the word of God *in* the words of scripture opens our heart to God's presence. We listen to a sentence, a story, or a parable not simply to be instructed, informed, or inspired but to be formed into a truly obedient person of faith. Listening in this way, we are guided by the Bible. The gospels are filled with examples of God's disclosure in the word. Personally, I am always touched by the story of Jesus in the synagogue of Nazareth. There he read from Isaiah, as it is recorded in Luke 4:18–19.

> The Spirit of the Lord is upon me,
> for he has anointed me
> to bring good news to the afflicted.
> He has sent me to proclaim liberty to the captives,
> sight to the blind,
> to let the oppressed go free,
> to proclaim a year of favor from the Lord.

After having read these words, Jesus said, "This text is fulfilled today even while you are listening." Contemplating this text, we suddenly see that the afflicted, the captives, the blind, and the oppressed are not people somewhere outside of the synagogue who, someday, will be liberated. They are the people—poor and needy—who are listening to Jesus here and now. You and I are captives in need of liberation, spiritually blind, and we want to see. You and I are the ones who feel oppressed and hope that Jesus will set us free.

To take the scriptures and read them contemplatively is called *lectio divina,* or spiritual reading. The term *lectio divina* comes from the Benedictine tradition and refers primarily to the divine or sacred reading of the Bible. *Lectio divina* is the ancient monastic practice of reading scripture meditatively—not to master the word, not to criticize the word, but to be mastered by and challenged by the word. It means to read the Bible "on your knees," that is, reverently, attentively, and with the deep conviction that God has a unique word for you in your own situation. In short, *spiritual reading is a reading in which we allow the word to read and interpret us.* Spiritual reading is the discipline of meditation on the word of God. To meditate means to "let the word descend from our minds into our hearts." Meditation means chewing on the word and incorporating it into our lives. It is the discipline by which we let the written word of God become a personal word for us, anchored in the center of our being.

Spiritual reading is food for our souls. We receive the word into our silence where we can ruminate on it, mull on it, digest it, and let it become flesh in us. In this way, *lectio divina* is the ongoing incarnation of God in our world.

Spiritual reading is the sacrament of the word, a participation in God's real presence.

Through regular spiritual practice, we develop an inner ear that allows us to recognize the Living Word in the written word, speaking directly to our most intimate needs and aspirations. In the spiritual reading of scripture, we focus on God and on God's words. We seek a word and then concentrate on that word in prayer. It is in the listening to particular words in the scripture that God suddenly becomes present to heal and save.

Reading often means gathering information, acquiring new insight and knowledge, and mastering a new field. It can lead us to degrees, diplomas, and certificates. Spiritual reading, however, is different. It means not simply reading about spiritual things but also reading about spiritual things in a spiritual way. That requires a willingness not just to read but to be read, not just to master but to be mastered by words. As long as we read the Bible or a spiritual book simply to acquire knowledge, our reading does not help us in our spiritual lives. We can become very knowledgeable about spiritual matters without becoming truly spiritual people.

Reading the word of God should lead us first of all to contemplation and meditation. As we read spiritually about spiritual things, we open our hearts to God's voice. Sometimes we must be willing to put down the book we are reading and just listen to what God is saying to us through its words.

Spiritual reading is far from easy in our modern, intellectual world, where we tend to make anything and everything we read subject to analysis and discussion. Instead of taking the words apart, we should bring them together in our innermost being; instead of wondering if we agree or disagree with what we have read, we should wonder which words are spoken directly to us and connect directly with our most personal story. Instead of thinking about the words as potential subjects for an interesting dialogue or paper, we should be willing to let them penetrate into the most hidden corners of our heart, even to those places where no other word has yet found entrance. Then and only then can the word bear fruit as seed sown in rich soil.

It helps to realize that the Bible is not primarily a book of information about God but of formation of the heart. It is not merely a book to be analyzed, scrutinized, and discussed, but a book to nurture, unify, and serve as a constant source of contemplation. We must struggle constantly against the temptation to read the Bible instrumentally as a book full of good stories and illustrations that can help us make our point in sermons, lectures, papers, and articles. The Bible does not speak to us as long as we want to use it. As long as we deal with the word of God as an item with which we can do many useful things, we don't really read the Bible or let it read us. Only when we are willing to hear the written word as a word for us can the Living Word disclose himself and penetrate into the center of our heart.

Lectio divina, then, involves a trust that in the words we read there is always the word of God to find. It is an attentive waiting for the words that connect deeply with the word, and a careful discerning of where the word is leading us. It is a form of listening in which we keep wondering which words are written for us as food for our own spiritual journey. Most important, it is a way of reading the word that is received with our whole being, our present condition, our past experiences, and our future aspirations. When we expose all that we are before the written word, the Living Word can be revealed here and now in our reading. When we read the Bible in this way, the Living Word found in the encounter between God's story and our individual story becomes written on our heart, where it enlivens us spiritually.

As we slowly let the written words enter into our minds and descend into our hearts, we become different people. The word gradually becomes flesh in us and transforms our whole being. In and through the reading of God's word and reflection on it, God becomes flesh in us now and makes us into living Christs for today.

Speaking the Word Out of Silence

A third way to encounter God in the word is through the *spoken word* (*rhema*), born out of silence, offered or received, as the ripe fruit of solitude.

The prophet Elijah, in the silence of the cave on Mount Horeb, heard the "still, small voice" of God (1 Kings 19:13). Jesus warned his listeners to be careful about the words they speak, "for by your words you will be judged" (Matthew 12:36–37). Paul refers to the spoken word of God as the "sword of the Spirit" (Ephesians 6:17). In Mark's Gospel (1:32–37) we read:

> Very early in the morning, while it was still dark, Jesus got up, left the house, and went off to a solitary place, where he prayed. Simon and his companions went to look for him, and when they found him, they exclaimed: "Everyone is looking for you!"
>
> Jesus replied, "Let us go somewhere else—to the nearby villages—so I can preach there also. That is why I have come."

There is little doubt that Jesus's life was a very busy life. He was busy teaching his disciples, preaching to the crowds, healing the sick, exorcising demons, responding to questions from foes and friends, and moving from one place to another. Jesus was so involved in activities that it became difficult to have any time alone. Yet he found a way to leave the crowd, withdraw from the pressing needs, and embrace solitude and silence. Alone with God in prayer, he could hear the spoken word directly from the heart of God. Solitary prayer was the source of his strength, the well of his wisdom, and the womb of his words. Having been in the presence of God, Jesus was able to discern God's will for the moment. After time set apart for solitude and silence, prayer and listening, he knew where to go, what to say, and what to do the rest of the day. "And he went all through Galilee, preaching in their synagogues and casting out demons" (Mark 1:38–39).

Consider the daily pattern and discipline of Jesus. "Early in the morning, while it was still dark, he got up, left the house, and went off to a solitary place, where he prayed." When do we get up, and where do we go, to be alone with God and pray? How do we know what to do and say on a particular day? Where do we go to find daily strength, gain wisdom from above, and hear a word from God?

In the Gospel of Luke we read about how Jesus goes up the mountain—with Peter, James, and John—to pray. There they see the face of Jesus change while he prays. His clothing becomes as bright as the sun, and a cloud overshadows them. They are afraid of what they see but are able to listen to the voice they hear say: "This is my Son, the Chosen One, listen to him" (Luke 9:28–36).

When Peter, James, and John see Jesus full of light on the mountain, they want that moment of clear vision to last forever. They hear a voice that reminds them of who Jesus is, and are told to listen to him. Their experience or vision is one of fullness of time (*kairos*) and a moment of grace.

As we listen to the word, there are moments when we experience complete unity within us and around us. In such moments of refreshment we are clear about our identity and calling. In such experiences we are most open to hear the still, small voice of God speak a personal word of hope and blessing to us in our heightened listening.

Here we glimpse the great mystery in which we participate through silence and the word, the mystery of God's own speaking. These moments are given to us so that we can remember the word when God seems far away and everything appears empty and useless. It is in the valleys that we need to remember the mountaintop. It is during the dry spells, when we are lonely or afraid, that we most need to listen to the word.

After we have been silent and listened, the time may come for us to speak. Silence teaches us when and how to speak a word of truth or wisdom to another. A powerful word is a word that emerges from silence, bears fruit, and returns to silence. It is a word that reminds us and others of the silence from which it comes and leads us back to that eternal silence. A word that is not rooted in silence is a weak, powerless word that sounds like a "clashing cymbal or a booming gong" (1 Corinthians 13:1).

Speaking the word of God from a place of silence is participating in God's own spoken word. It is speaking what is heard out of eternity into time. It is a speaking that emerges out of silent love and thus creates new life. When our words are no longer connected with and nurtured by the silence from which they come, they lose their authority and degenerate into "mere words" that cannot bear fruit. But when our words carry within them God's eternal silence, then they can be truly life-giving.

Let me give you an example: If you too quickly say to a person in pain, "God loves you as the apple of his eye; God is always with you even when you feel most alone," such words can be little more than pious phrases that do more harm than good. But when these same words are spoken from a heart that has listened long to God's voice and has gradually been molded by it, then they can truly bring new life and healing. Then, words are *sacramental*—they carry within themselves the reality to which they point.

Sometimes we need to hear a life-giving word spoken by another and addressed to our current condition. God sometimes sends a prophet to speak a personal word to us in time of need. Often, for example, parishioners say to their pastors: "I felt you were speaking God's word directly to me today in your sermon." Sometimes the needed word comes straight to our heart directly from God. More often, it is in the loving words of others that we hear God's word for us.

There have been many occasions in my life during which I felt isolated and cut off from God and from my fellow human beings. It was during these times that I heard God speak to me through someone who spoke a word with great humility and love. When I received it, a safe space was opened in me where I could meet my God and my brothers and sisters in a new way. Every time this happened I felt a deep desire to let that word grow deeper by dwelling in its silence.

Silence is the royal road to spiritual formation. Without silence, the spoken word can never bear fruit. Moreover, only through silence can the word descend from the mind into the heart. As long as our hearts and minds are filled with words of our own making, there is no space for the word to enter deeply into our heart and take root.

All spoken words need to be born out of silence and constantly return to it. Silence gives strength and fruitfulness to the word. Out of silence the word within can be spoken. Our spoken words are meant to disclose the mystery of the silence from which they come. Once words complete their function, the silence remains. The Taoist philosopher Chuang Tzu expresses this well:

The purpose of a fish trap is to catch fish, and when the fish are caught, the trap is forgotten. The purpose of a rabbit snare is to catch rabbits. When the rabbits are caught, the snare is forgotten. The purpose of the word is to convey ideas. When the ideas are grasped, the words are forgotten. Where can I find someone who has forgotten words? That is the one I would like to talk to.[29]

WRITING THE WORD

For me, to find God in the word often requires writing. Spiritual writing has a very important place in spiritual formation. Even so, writing often is the source of great pain and anxiety. It is remarkable how hard it is to sit down quietly and trust our own creativity. There seems to be a deep-seated resistance to writing. I have experienced this resistance myself over and over again. Even after many years of writing, I experience real fear when I face the empty page. Why am I so afraid? Sometimes I have an imaginary reader in mind who is looking over my shoulder and rejecting every word I write down. Sometimes I am overwhelmed by the countless books and articles that already have been written and I cannot imagine that I have anything to say that hasn't already been said better by someone else. Sometimes it seems that every sentence fails to express what I really want to say and that written words simply cannot hold what goes on in my mind and heart. These fears sometimes paralyze me and make me delay or even abandon my writing plans.

And still, every time I overcome these fears and trust not only my own unique way of being in the world but also my ability to give words to it, I experience a deep spiritual satisfaction. I have been trying to understand the nature of this satisfaction. What I am gradually discovering is that in the writing I come in touch with the Spirit of God within me and experience how I am led to new places.

Many think that writing means writing down ideas, insights, or visions. They are of the opinion that they first must have something to say before they can put it on paper. For them, writing is little more than recording preexistent thoughts. But with this approach, true writing is impossible. Writing is a process in which we discover what lives in us. The writing itself reveals to us what is alive in us. The deepest satisfaction of writing is precisely that it opens up new spaces within us of which we were not aware before we started to write. To write is to embark on a journey of which we do not know the final destination. Thus, writing requires a great act of trust. We have to say to ourselves: "I do not yet know what I carry in my heart, but I trust that it will emerge as I write." Writing is like giving away the few loaves and fishes we have, trusting that they will multiply in the giving. Once we dare to "give away" on paper the few thoughts that come to us, we start discovering how much is hidden underneath these thoughts and thus we gradually come in touch with our own riches and resources.

Spiritual formation requires a constant attempt to identify ways in which God is present among us. Regular writing is one important way to do this. I remember how, during a long stay in Latin America, daily writing helped me to discern how the Spirit of God was at work in all that I was experiencing. Underneath the seemingly fragmenting multitude of visual and mental stimulations, I was able to discover a "hidden wholeness." Writing made that possible. It brought me in touch with the unity underneath the diversity and the solid current beneath the restless waves. Writing became the way to stay in touch with the faithfulness of God in the midst of a chaotic existence.

In these circumstances I came to realize that writing was indeed a form of prayer. It also brought about community, since the written word helped me to create a space where different people, who found it hard to identify anything lasting among their passing impressions, could gather and come to trust their own experiences. These words became a proclamation of God's faithful presence even there where least expected.

Finally, let me share with you an example of how spiritual writing—a simple letter—revealed a word of hope to someone in need:

There was a Dutch soldier who was captured and made a prisoner of war. The enemies took him far away from his homeland, and he was completely isolated from his family and friends. He did not hear anything from home and felt very lonely and afraid. He did not know if anybody at home was alive or how his country was doing. He had a thousand questions but could not answer a single one. He felt he did not have anything left to live for and was in despair.

Then, he got an unexpected letter, crumpled and dirty because it had traveled so long and far to reach him. It was just a piece of paper, but precious to him because of the words it might contain. He opened the letter and read these simple words: "We all are waiting for you at home. Everything is fine. Do not worry. We will see you back at home and we all desire to see you."

This simple letter changed his life. He suddenly felt better and no longer despaired. There was a reason to live. The external circumstances of his life, his imprisonment and isolation, did not change. He continued his labor, endured the same difficult things, but he felt completely different on the inside. Somebody was waiting for him, and desired to see him. He still had a home. Hope was reborn in him that day. Writing simple words in a short letter saved a life, for there was a word of God in the words of another.

What I am trying to say is that God has written us a love letter in the scripture, the written word. The written word points to the Living Word, which is God incarnate in the person of Jesus. In both the Living Word and the written word, God continues to speak—personally and in a quiet voice. We speak the word of God to each other out of the silence of listening to God. And writing the word also reveals the word of God to us and others. Thus, a personal relationship with the *Living Word,* contemplative reading of the *written word,* silent meditation before a *spoken word* is offered or received, and the spiritual act of *writing a word* in a letter or prayer journal are four ways we hear the word of God. Or, to put it another way, we encounter God in the word through the disciplines of obedient listening, sacred reading, humble speaking, and spiritual writing.

GOING DEEPER: EXERCISES FOR SPIRITUAL DIRECTION

FINDING GOD IN THE WORD

Listening, reading, speaking, and writing in ways that are faithful to the word of God are difficult spiritual disciplines. Here are four simple rules for finding God in the word:

Listen to the *Living Word*, which is Jesus, in your heart through contemplative prayer.

Read the *written word* with an open embrace through the practice of *lectio divina*.

Let your speaking of a word be born out of a gentle silence and humbleness of heart.

After a time or prayer and mediation, write a love letter or a spiritual reflection about what God may be saying. Share this with your spiritual director or prayer group.

With Christ in our hearts, the Bible in our hands, and some time for solitude and silence in our lives, we can find God in the word. The Living Word of God draws us into silence, and silence makes us attentive to God's written word, but word and silence both need the guidance of a spoken word through a trusted friend. May I be your guide for a moment? I want to lead you through a spiritual exercise of centering prayer, *lectio divina*, and spiritual writing to help you find God in the word.[30]

Centering Prayer

First, bring yourself to God as you are. Sit comfortably, your Bible open to a selected reading. All you have to bring to your relationship with God is yourself. The object is not to try to feel special or holy, but to feel plainly yourself.

Then, close your eyes and become quietly attentive to yourself. . . . Become aware of your breathing, and begin to relax with its natural rhythm.

As you relax, you will first become aware of noises, smells . . . soon your quiet will be interrupted, first by a trickle, then a rush of thoughts, feelings, shopping lists, things undone, pressing concerns.

Allow these to come. They are not obstacles to this time of quiet, they are its purpose.

Resist concentrating on any particular thought or feeling (this will block others), but allow each one to pass on by. When you do become hooked by one, don't fight. Become attentive once again to your breathing, and then allow the thoughts and feelings to come again.

You will often find that the rush subsides to a few deeper thoughts, thicker feelings. Listen . . . Listen . . . Listen . . .

After several minutes, when you are ready, open your eyes. You are now ready to seek God in the written word.

Lectio Divina

Choose a passage of scripture to read aloud, slowly, attentively, once through. Pause to let the passage sink in. Resist a familiar understanding, even of a familiar passage. Allow yourself to hear the story anew.

Reread the passage, piece by piece. Note the story line and questions raised. Again, resist the familiar interpretation. Look for a word or two in the story. Explore the passage the way a child might explore a strange room, in the spirit of curiosity and openness.

Read the passage a third time. What word or words jump out at you, commanding your attention? Stay with that word as long as you can. Meditate on it. Chew on it. Is God speaking a personal word to you today? Contemplate the personal word for you today in the written word. Live today in the joy that the Living Word has spoken to you.

Spiritual Writing

When time allows, open your journal and record your spiritual insights.

Start by reviewing and reflecting upon the particular circumstances of your life today. What are the challenges of the day? Important opportunities that lie before you? Decisions that need to be made?

As you reflect, reconsider the scripture and the words that commanded your attention through *lectio divina*. How do these words and images connect to your life today? How is the biblical story a part of your story? How do its questions connect with your own questions?

How does God come to you as you listen to the word? Where do you discern the healing hand of God touching you through the word? How are your sadness, your grief, and your mourning being transformed at this very moment through the word? Do you sense the fire of God's love purifying your heart and giving you new life?

As thoughts come to you, jot them down on paper—perhaps just a word or two at first, then phrases or sentences as your reflections become more developed. Try to capture specifics rather than just general themes.

You may find that in response to new insights, new ways of acting in familiar situations present themselves. In the same way, you may be troubled by portions of scripture that leave you confused, uneasy, with a feeling of dissonance. These can prove to be as valuable, in ways that are not immediately obvious, as those portions that are more obviously related. Note them as well.

When the time has come to end your quiet time, be refreshed. When ready, close with a prayer, perhaps the Lord's Prayer, spoken slowly, bearing in mind the questions and insights that have come to you today. Give thanks. Invite God's presence into your life's movements this coming day, bearing with you the fruits of your time apart.

With any discipline, such as playing an instrument or learning a language, beginnings are awkward. Stay with it. Give it time and practice, and the artificiality of the discipline will fade, giving way to familiarity and fluency.

CLOSING PRAYER

O Lord Jesus, your words to your Father were born out of your silence. Lead me into this silence, so that my words may be spoken in your name and thus be fruitful. It is so hard to be silent, silent with my mouth, but even more, silent with my heart. There is so much talking going on within me. . . . If I were simply to rest at your feet and realize that I belong to you and you alone, I would easily stop arguing with all the real and imaginary people around me. . . . I know that in the silence of my heart you will speak to me and show me your love. Give me, O Lord, that silence. Let me be patient and grow slowly into this silence in which I can be with you. Amen.

REFLECT AND JOURNAL:

Read Mark 1:35–37 slowly and then let it read you for a few moments. Journal about your experience of being read by the word.

Write a love letter to yourself from God. What do you know about God's love for you?

PART THREE

Look to Others in

Community

EIGHT
Where Do I Belong?

AN OLD Hasidic tale summarizes the need to move from solitude to community in the spiritual life in order to find our true home in the world:

~Darkness and the Dawn~

The rabbi asked his students: "How can we determine the hour of dawn, when the night ends and the day begins?"

One of the rabbi's students suggested: "When from a distance you can distinguish between a dog and a sheep?"

"No," was the answer of the rabbi.

"It is when one can distinguish between a fig tree and a grapevine?" asked a second student.

"No," the rabbi said.

"Please tell us the answer then," said the students.

"It is then," said the wise teacher, "when you can look into the face of another human being and you have enough light in you to recognize your brother or your sister. Until then it is night, and darkness is still with us."[31]

The spiritual journey moves us from solitude to community and to ministry as we follow Jesus. This movement is exemplified in the beautiful story of Jesus and his disciples in Luke 6:12–19; this story of relationship begins in solitude at night, moves to community building in the morning, and ends in active ministry in the afternoon:

> Jesus went out to a mountainside to pray, and spent the *night* praying to God. When *morning* came, he called his disciples to him and chose twelve of them, whom he also designated apostles. . . . He went down with them and stood on a level place. A large crowd of his disciples was there and a great number of people from all over . . . who had come to hear him and to be healed of their diseases. Those troubled by evil spirits were cured, and the people all tried to touch him, because power was coming from him and healing them all [emphasis added].

Jesus spent time on the mountain at night in solitary prayer. He came down in the morning and formed his community. Then, in the afternoon, with his apostles, he went out and healed the sick and proclaimed the good news. I've been fascinated by the sequence of prayer at night, community in the morning, ministry in the afternoon. Notice the order—from solitude to community to ministry. The night is for solitude, the morning for community, the afternoon for ministry. *Night, morning,* and *afternoon* are symbols for the movement from solitude to community to ministry that Jesus lived out. These are the three disciplines we are called to practice on the long journey home:

(1) solitude or communion with God in prayer; (2) recognizing and gathering together in community; and (3) ministry or compassion in the world.

GROUNDED IN SOLITUDE

How do we learn to be in solitude with God? In Rembrandt's painting *The Return of the Prodigal Son*, the father holds his returning child and touches his child in a loving embrace. With his son safe within his outstretched arms, the father's expression seems to say to me: "I'm not going to ask you any questions. Wherever you have gone, whatever you have done, and whatever people say about you, you're my beloved child. I hold you safe in my embrace. I hug you. I gather you under my wings. You can come home to me."

In solitude and silent communion with God in prayer, I have to kneel before the Father, just as the prodigal son did upon his return, and put my ear against his chest and listen, without interruption, to the heartbeat of God. Similarly, in solitude and silence, I am drawn to communion with God in prayer. If we take the time to be still, we will be led to an inner place, a place within us where God has chosen to dwell, a place where we are held safe in the embrace of the all-loving One who calls us by name.

Jesus says, "Anyone who loves me will keep my word and my Father will love him, and we shall come to him and make our home in him." I am God's home! Yes, God dwells in my innermost being, but how do I accept Jesus's call: "Make your home in me as I make my home in you." The invitation is clear and unambiguous. To make my home where God has made his home is a great spiritual challenge.

Intimate communion with God is not an easy discipline. Remember, Jesus spent the night in prayer. Night is a time of mystery, darkness, solitude, and sometimes loneliness. Night is a symbol of the fact that prayer is not something you always feel. It's not a voice you always hear with your physical ears. Prayer doesn't always offer an insight that suddenly comes to your mind. Communion with God is more often an intuition or inner conviction that God's heart is greater than your heart, God's mind is greater than your human mind, and God's light is so much greater than your light that it might blind you and make you feel like you're in the night.

To practice solitude we must each claim regular time to quiet ourselves physically and spiritually. Start with a few minutes a day—perhaps in the early morning when the heat and light of the day have not yet arrived, or in the late evening when they have begun to dissipate. This is a time for wordless prayer or focused prayer through journaling or sacred reading followed by open space to listen for God's voice or a sense of God's presence or a call to wait. Truly, the dawn or twilight hours are ideal times for solitude and prayer that grounds us in God and prepares us to live with and love others. Communion with God is where spiritual community begins.

WHEN SOLITUDE GREETS SOLITUDE

When the morning comes, solitude greets solitude and community is formed. It's remarkable that solitude always calls us to community. In solitude, you come to know yourself as vulnerable and broken, yet beloved by God. In solitude, you realize that you are part of a human family and that you want to be together with others. The symbol of the dawn is the awareness that we are all related, connected, and interdependent. As the wise rabbi in the parable taught his students: until "you can look into the face of another human being and you have enough light in you to recognize your brother or your sister . . . it is night, and darkness is still with us."

By forming community, I don't mean creating formal communities. Community as a place of spiritual belonging happens in families, friendships, churches, parishes, twelve-step programs, and prayer groups. Community does not require an organization or institution; community is a way of living and relating: you gather around people with whom you want to proclaim the truth that we are the beloved sons and daughters of God. "Wherever two or three are gathered in my name," Jesus said, "I am there in your midst" (Matthew 18:20). For me, community has been most authentic in a Eucharistic faith community, and specifically for me this was L'Arche Daybreak. For you, community may be found in your local church or prayer group. However you define a faith community, it is your spiritual home.

Home is not always comfortable, and community is not easy. In every community the healing of acceptance happens and deep betrayals take place. Our humanity with all of its splendor and the hurt of pain emerges. In the Gospel of Luke, Jesus identifies his community of twelve disciples one by one, including "Judas Iscariot, who became a traitor" (Luke 6:16). Betrayal means to break trust. A traitor means to "hand over." There is always someone in the community who betrays your trust or hands you over to something painful or unwanted. As soon as you have community, you have a problem. Someone once said that "community is the place where the person you least want to live with always lives." That person who annoys you or who needs too much is always in your community somewhere.

But it's not just one person who does the betraying. In the eyes of others, I may be that person. Or you may be that person. It's not that one person in the community is the problem; it's more that different people are handing other people over to suffering all the time without even wanting to or knowing what they are doing. There is always someone who doesn't satisfy my need or someone who irritates me. Community is not some sentimental ideal place or time where everybody lives together, loves each other, and always gets along. That's never going to happen. Rather, in living together we come to realize that community doesn't require or offer total emotional harmony. It offers us the context where we try to love one another and receive the love and care of others.

Why is it so important that solitude comes before community, that community springs forth from solitude? If we do not know we are the beloved sons and daughters of God, we're going to expect someone in the community to make us feel special and worthy. Ultimately, they cannot. If we start with trying to create community, we'll expect someone to give us that perfect, unconditional love. But true community is not loneliness grabbing onto loneliness: "I'm so lonely, and you're so lonely; why don't we get together." Many relationships begin out of a fear of being alone, but they can't ultimately satisfy a need that only solitude with God can fulfill. *Community is solitude greeting solitude:* "I am the beloved; you are the beloved; together we can build a home or place of welcome together." Sometimes you feel close, and that's wonderful. Sometimes you don't feel much love, and that's hard. But we can be faithful to one another in community. We can build a home together and create space for God and for others in the household of God.

Though it's not easy, Jesus calls us to live together as a family of faith and commitment. In community we learn what it means to confess our weakness and to forgive each other. In community we discover what it means to let go of our self-will and to really live for others. In community we learn true humility. People of faith need community, for without it we become individualistic and, at times, egocentric. As difficult as it is, community is not really an option in the spiritual life. Community springs forth from solitude, and without a community, communion with God is impossible. We are called to God's table together, not by ourselves. Spiritual formation, therefore, always includes formation to life in community. We all have to find our way home to God in solitude and in community with others.

How I Found My Way Home

When I was asked to come to Yale, I was forty years old, and my bishop said I could go for a few years; I stayed ten. I was doing well on the level of my ambitions, but I began to question whether I was really doing God's will. Was I being obedient? Was I the priest I wanted to be? Was Yale really my home?

I prayed: "God, you know what I should do. Let me know, and I will follow you. I will go anywhere you want. But you have to be very clear about it." In 1981 I suddenly had this feeling that I wanted to go to Latin America and work with the poor. I relinquished my professorship at Yale and began preparing for a pilgrimage to Bolivia and Peru. Friends wondered whether I was doing the wise thing. I didn't have much support.

Quickly I discovered that being a missionary in Latin America was not my vocation. It was hard to be there. People were good to me, welcoming, remarkably hospitable. But God did not call me there. I was driven there. I spent some time with Gustavo Gutierrez, who did not encourage me to stay there. "Maybe they need you more at the university to talk about Latin America," he said. "Do reverse mission to the first world from the third world, and write." Sadly, the poor in Peru did not become family, nor did Latin America become my heart's home.

Meanwhile, Harvard Divinity School asked me to join their faculty. I did so, and tried to teach about the spiritual struggles of people in Latin America and the need for social justice there. But the students felt an enormous need to talk about prayer and contemplation. They asked me about the inner spiritual life and the ministry. I liked teaching at Harvard, and I made some beautiful friends there. At the same time, I didn't feel Harvard was a safe place for me. It was too much podium, too much publicity, too public. Too many people came to listen for an intellectual understanding rather than spiritual insight. It was an intensely competitive place, an intellectual battleground. Harvard was not home. I needed a place where I could pray more. I needed to be in a community where my spiritual life would deepen in relationship to others.

My decision to leave Harvard was a difficult one. For many months I was not sure if I would be following or betraying my vocation by leaving. The outer voices kept saying: "You can do so much good here. People need you!" The inner voices kept saying, "What good is it to preach the gospel to others while losing your own soul?" Finally, I realized that my increasing darkness, my feelings of rejection, my inordinate need for affirmation and affection, and my deep sense of not belonging were clear signs that I was not following the way of God's spirit. The fruits of the spirit are not sadness, loneliness, and separation, but joy, solitude, community, and ministry. As soon as I left Harvard I felt so much inner freedom, so much joy and new energy, that I could look back on my former life as a prison in which I had locked myself.

I did not know where to go, except that I had a deep connection with Jean Vanier and his L'Arche community in France. So I went there for a year of discernment of my calling and what community might become a home for me. Again, I prayed: "God, what do you want me to do?" Before the year was over, I got a letter from the Daybreak community in Canada—one of over one hundred communities throughout the world where children, men, and women with disabilities and those who assist them live together. They were calling me to become a member of the community and to be their priest. It was the first time in my whole life that I felt called to anything. All the other times, it had been my initiative. This time I felt God was calling me. I wondered if this letter was the answer to my prayer.

At the end of August 1986, I moved to Daybreak, into the New House, where six handicapped people—Rose, Adam, Bill, John, Trevor, and Raymond—and their four assistants welcomed me warmly. Friendships gradually developed with all the members of the house. But these bonds of friendship were not without great cost. I had to face the cost of recognizing my own handicaps! I had always known they were there, but I had always been able to keep them out of sight. But those who cannot hide their handicaps do not allow the assistants to hide theirs either. I was offered much support and guidance during my first months as I lived through my own fears and insecurities. Self-confrontation was the hardest battle of all.

The L'Arche community gradually became my home. Never in my life did I dream that men and women with a mental handicap would be the ones who would put their hands on me in a gesture of blessing and offer me a home. For a long time I had sought safety and security among the wise and clever, hardly aware that the things of the Kingdom are revealed to "little children," that God has chosen "those who by human standards are fools to shame the wise." But when I experienced the warm, unpretentious reception of those who have nothing to boast about and experienced a loving embrace from people who didn't ask any questions, I began to discover that a true spiritual homecoming means a return to the poor in spirit to whom the Kingdom of Heaven belongs. The embrace of the Father became very real to me in the embraces of the physically and mentally poor.

Over the years at Daybreak I found the community to be full of love and support, and also hard to endure. Life in community did not keep the darkness away. To the contrary. It seems that the light that attracted me to L'Arche also made me conscious of the darkness in myself. In community, you really come to know yourself. Jealousy, anger, the feeling of being rejected or neglected, the sense of not truly belonging—all these emerged in the context of a community striving for a life of forgiveness, reconciliation, and healing.

LIFE TOGETHER IN COMMUNITY

Community life opened me up to the real spiritual combat: the struggle to keep moving toward the light precisely when the darkness is so real. For example, sometimes in community I put claims on people that are so high that nobody can live up to them—emotional claims and expectations of which I am not fully aware. I expect someone to take away my loneliness. I expect that person to give me a sense of at-homeness. I expect that when we live together, everything will be joyful and pleasant. I expect the community always to be a peaceful living together with no hard work or conflict. When my expectations are not realized, I am left feeling upset, lonely, and depressed. Why are my expectations of others so high? What need in me is not being addressed or fulfilled?

These questions lead me back to prayer and to the need for spiritual direction in my spiritual life and in my community relationships. I am reminded of how important it is that solitude precedes community and that family life is recognized as inherently difficult. Once solitude is embraced, I have learned that forgiveness and celebration can come to characterize authentic community even with its challenges.

COMMUNITY REQUIRES FORGIVENESS

Within the discipline of life in community are the twin gifts of forgiveness and celebration that need to be opened and used regularly. What is forgiveness? *Forgiveness means that I continually am willing to forgive the other person for not fulfilling all my needs and desires.* Forgiveness says, "I know you love me, but you don't have to love me unconditionally, because only God can do that." I too must ask forgiveness for not being able to fulfill other people's total needs, for no human being can do that.

We all have wounds. We all live in pain and disappointment. We all have feelings of loneliness that lurk beneath all our successes, feelings of uselessness that hide under all the praise, feelings of meaninglessness even when people say we are fantastic—and that is what makes us sometimes grab onto people and expect from them affection, affirmation, and love that they cannot give. If we want other people to give us something that only God can give, we are guilty of idolatry. We say, "Love me!" and before long we become demanding and manipulative. It's so important that we keep forgiving one another—not once in a while but every moment of life. This is what makes community possible, when we can come together in a forgiving and undemanding way.

Our heart longs for satisfaction, for total communion. But human beings, whether it's your husband, your wife, your father, mother, brother, sister, or child, are all limited in giving the level of love and acceptance we all crave. But since we want so much and we get only part of what we want, we have to keep on forgiving people for not giving us all we want. So, I forgive you since you can only love me in a limited way. I forgive my mother that she is not everything I would like her to be. I forgive my father because he did the best he could. This is of enormous importance right now because constantly people look to blame their parents, their friends, and the church for not giving them what they need. Many people are so angry. They cannot forgive people for offering only limited expressions of an unlimited love. God's love is unlimited; our love is not. Any relationship you enter into—in communion, friendship, marriage, community, or church—will always be riddled with frustration and disappointment. So forgiveness becomes the word for divine love in the human context.

❋

Community is not possible without the willingness to forgive one another "seventy-seven times" (Matthew 18:22). Forgiveness is the cement of community life. Forgiveness holds us all together through good and bad times, and it allows us to grow in mutual love.

As people who have hearts that long for perfect love, we have to forgive one another for not being able to give or receive that perfect love in our everyday lives. Our many needs constantly interfere with our desire to be there for the other unconditionally. Our love is always limited by spoken or unspoken conditions. What needs to be forgiven? *We need to forgive one another for not being God!*

Let me share a personal story that illustrates this truth. Shortly after I arrived at Daybreak, it seemed to me that God had given me a wonderful gift of love and special friendship. As this relationship grew and developed, I became very attached to a male friend. Looking back, I was overly attached and needy and had to let go, forgive, and be forgiven. I wrote a book about this called *The Inner Voice of Love.*

My friend Nathan had a surprising capability to open up a place in me that had been closed, and I focused all of my emotional needs on him. I became very dependent on him, which prevented me from making God and the community the true center of my life. In his presence I felt fully alive and loved, and I did not want to let him go. At a certain point, he could no longer hold on to me, and he said, "I no longer want to be with you. Whenever I'm with you, there is so much pressure. You want to be right with me all the time."

Here was a person who really understood and loved me, who brought me in touch with important walled-off parts of myself, and who then abruptly ended the friendship. Well, I just broke down, totally broke down. I slipped into a terrible depression. I was totally paralyzed—I couldn't do ministry and was on the edge of despair—so I had to leave my community for several months and stay in a therapeutic center.

The clinical psychiatrist I saw dispassionately said, "It is very simple: you got infatuated with somebody, that person dropped you, you are depressed. It will take six months of grieving to get over it. Be sure you never see this person again, and it'll all be fine. You are normal. On the scale in our psychiatric handbook, your neurosis is a number 2." He seemed like a horse doctor to me.

When he said that it would take six months and that I would have to leave my community and never see this person again, I reacted negatively. He said that I never should have been a celibate because I obviously get very attached to people, so it isn't positive. I just didn't buy it. I said to the psychiatrist, "I'm not going to keep seeing you. You have me all figured out, my pain is all so simple to you, and I'm not going to see you anymore."

I knew I had to forgive my dear friend for not being for me what I thought I needed. I could say it a thousand times, but my emotions weren't there. I couldn't forgive for a long time. I felt so angry, so rejected, so depressed, because my closest friend thought I was intolerable to live with?

Gradually, I was able to forgive my friend for not loving me fully as only God can. I had to forgive him for not being God! It wasn't an intellectual task, but a matter of the heart. It was an enormous opportunity to grow into the truth of knowing that only God can give me what I want from another person.

I knew in my heart that what I experienced was a God-given relationship, that the love was real, that I experienced something that was extremely important. I knew that I didn't have to leave my community, that the relationship could be healed and restored, and that together we could work it through. And I knew that I did not have to renounce my calling as a celibate priest in order to find fulfillment. In the beginning I did not see or say all that clearly. But when the pain diminished, I reclaimed myself and returned home.

I don't deny the infatuation part of this crisis; I don't want to make it sound only spiritual, yet it was God's way of calling me to claim my belovedness and embodiment as a human being, to listen to that voice and hear God say, "I love you with an unconditional love. With or without a particular person in your life, I am with you and I am what you need. In your weakness, you would have turned to him; instead you came to me."

It was very important that my community did not abandon me but supported me in this crisis. They sent me to that therapeutic center and came to visit me. When I felt worthless, I generalized it to say, nobody cares. The opposite, of course, was true. Community members said, "Just because your friend can no longer be with you doesn't mean we don't love you. We love you a lot. You're very important to us." I didn't believe it at first and felt their love was very superficial. In retrospect, I don't think I would have survived without them.

After all the pain and struggle to forgive and let go, a miracle of reconciliation occurred in our community. Not only was I able to reestablish contact with my friend, but our relationship over time was healed and restored. Finally, Nathan recognized that I was no longer projecting all my needs, and we again became very good friends.

FORGIVENESS LEADS TO CELEBRATION

The interesting thing is that when you can forgive people for not being God, then you can celebrate that they are a reflection of God, a reflection of God's great unconditional love. You can say, "I love you because you have such beautiful gifts of God's love," or, "You cannot give what only God can give, but what you have to offer is worth celebrating." You can say, "Wow, that's beautiful!"

To celebrate each other's gifts does not mean giving each other little compliments—"You are so good at singing." No, that's a talent show. To celebrate another's gift means to accept that person's full humanity as a reflection of God.

By "celebrate" I mean to lift up, affirm, confirm, and rejoice in another person's gifts and graces as reflections of God's unlimited gift of love and grace. A husband or wife can do so much, but then you also need your community. The community is in a way a mosaic: every person is a little piece of a different color, and together all the pieces show us the face of God. But each little piece on its own is a very limited reflection of that great love.

Celebration is a very concrete expression of love. A birthday celebration, for example, simply says, "I'm happy you are here." It doesn't mean lifting up people's talents, as in "You're a good piano player." You are not more gifted because you can play the piano better than I can. That's just a talent. Your greater gift may be your capacity for bringing joy and peace into a room with your music. Celebration means lifting up people's gifts of joy, peace, love, perseverance, kindness, gentleness. We lift up the gifts of the Spirit—for these are the reflections of God.

I have learned so much since coming to Daybreak. I've learned that my real gifts are not that I write books or that I taught at universities. My real gifts are discovered by and reflected back to me through community members who know me and love me well. Sometimes they say to me: "Henri, you give good advice. Why don't you read some of your own books?" At other times, I find healing in being known and celebrated in my weakness and vulnerability. Suddenly I realize that I'm a good person in the eyes of people who don't read my books and don't care about my successes. These people can forgive me for my little egocentric gestures and behaviors that are always there.

In my community we have to do a lot of forgiving. But right in the midst of forgiving springs a celebration. With forgiveness and celebration, community becomes the place where we call forth the gifts of other people, lift them up, and say, "You are the beloved daughter and the beloved son. With you I am well pleased."

CONNECTED THROUGH LOVE

Thus, when you discover your belovedness by God in solitude, you see the belovedness of other people in community and can call that beauty forth in ministry. It's an incredible mystery of God's love that the more you know you are loved, the more you will see how deeply your sisters and your brothers in the human family are loved. The more you love others without conditions, the more you can love yourself the way God loves you and others. And the more you are loved by others, the more you realize how much you are the beloved of God. Finding your way home is learning how all love is connected, expressed, and lived out in community. As St. John so eloquently wrote: "Beloved, let us love one another, for love comes from God. Everyone who loves has been born of God and knows God. Whoever does not love does not know God, because God is love" (1 John 4:7–8).

GOING DEEPER:
EXERCISES FOR SPIRITUAL
DIRECTION

The spiritual life can never be separated from a life together. True prayer, even the most intimate prayer, always leads to new connections with others. More than sermons, lectures, or individual reading, being together in a common search for God can deepen and broaden our life in the Spirit. The following principles may prove helpful in creating community and group formation:

PRINCIPLES FOR COMMUNITY-BUILDING

Leadership always is an issue in small groups or larger communities of faith. What form of leadership are you most comfortable with? Which leadership models do you find most challenging?

Remember, the primary purpose of community is to learn together about the life of the Spirit of God within and among us through prayer, support, and accountability. Rational analysis, interpersonal dynamics, intellectual discussion, and debate, while helpful in overcoming temporary obstacles, are not the primary spiritual tasks of a community of faith.

In order to find the right "wavelength" for group interaction, the word of God needs to be the center of our meetings. Concretely, this means that there should be no community meetings without reading scripture together. A good way to do this is for different members of the group to read the text slowly and loudly and for everyone else to listen with great reverence for the word.

Besides listening together to the word of God, it seems crucial that a good period of time be spent in silence. Being together in a prayerful silence during which the word can enter more deeply into our hearts can become one of the most community-forming experiences possible.

Speaking may be one of the most difficult things to do in both small groups and larger communities. We are so used to agreeing, disagreeing, arguing, and debating that we have often forgotten the language that helps us to build community and to recognize the mystery of the Spirit among us. Therefore, let our words be few. Let our lives loom large.

REFLECT AND JOURNAL:

Who is in your faith community? What binds you together? What makes your community a challenge?

Who do you need to forgive for not being God?

NINE
How Can I Be of Service?

AN OLD legend in the Talmud suggests where to begin when searching for a way to be of service in the world:

~Where to Find the Messiah?~

Rabbi Yoshua ben Levi asked Elijah the prophet, "When will Messiah come?"

Elijah replied, "Go and ask him yourself."

"Where is he?"

"Sitting at the gates of the city."

"How shall I know him?"

"He is sitting among the poor covered with wounds. The others unbind all their wounds at the same time and then bind them up again. But he unbinds one at a time and binds it up again, saying to himself, 'Perhaps I shall be needed: if so I must always be ready so as not to delay for a moment.'"[32]

This story raises many questions, such as: How does the prophet know when the Messiah will come or where he might be found? Why would the Messiah be found outside the gates of the city? Why sitting among the poor? Why covered with wounds? Why changing bandages, others' and his own, one at a time?

The coming Messiah, according to the prophets, is a suffering servant and wounded healer (see Isaiah 53). His place is among the poor. He tends to his own wounds as well as the wounds of others, in anticipation of the moment when he will be needed. So it is with all ministers and servants of God. We are called to be wounded healers who look after our own wounds and at the same time prepare to heal the wounds of others.

How can you be of service in the world, you ask? What is your ministry to others? Where are you to spend your life energies? In this chapter, I want to answer those questions by exploring the healing ministry of Jesus, the practice of compassion and gratitude in community, and, finally, how to follow Jesus on his downward path through voluntary displacement.

THE HEALING MINISTRY OF JESUS

In Luke 8:42–48, we read:

> As Jesus was on his way, the crowds almost crushed him. And a woman was there who had been subject to bleeding for twelve years, but no one could heal her. She came up behind him and touched the edge of his cloak, and immediately her bleeding stopped.

"Who touched me?" Jesus asked. When they all denied
it, Peter said, "Master, the people are crowding and pressing
against you."

But Jesus said, "Someone touched me; I know that
power has gone out from me."

Then the woman, seeing that she could not go unno-
ticed, came trembling and fell at his feet. . . . Then Jesus
said to her, "Daughter, your faith has healed you. Go in
peace."

Jesus did not cure the crowds applying proven ministry techniques. He spoke from his heart, acted out of compassion, and left
the results to God. He wanted only one thing—to do the will of his
Father. He didn't say, "Let me talk to you for ten minutes, and maybe
I can do something about this." He didn't sit people down and di-
agnose them and say, "I can help *you*, but I can't help *you*." Jesus was
always listening and in touch with God, and out of his intimacy with
God there was a power that radiated out to everyone.

"Whatever I do, you can do also, even greater things," Jesus said
(see John 14:12). "Go out and heal the sick. Walk on the snake. Call
the dead to life." This was not small talk. He said it precisely: "You
are sent into the world just as I was sent into the world—to heal and
cure" (Mark 16:15–18). We have to trust in God's healing power. Trust
that if we are living as the beloved and have compassion for people,
many will be healed, whether or not we notice it at the time.

The question in ministry is not "How do I bring all these people
to Jesus?" or "How do I make these people believe?" or "How do I
help all these people?" Ministry happens. You and I *do* very little. I
don't try to get people to go to church or to join me in prayer and the

Eucharist. I just start to pray and offer Eucharist and see who comes. I'm not concerned with fixing the marriage of the one who is considering divorce or convincing the woman who doesn't believe in Jesus to have faith. I'm here to say this is who I am, and this is who God is for me, and to be there for others. You have to trust that if you are the son or daughter of God, a healing power will go out from you and people will be healed. People will want to know where your energy comes from. They will want to touch you to get the overflow.

All followers of Jesus are called to ministry. That's the whole concept of the Christian church: we are the body of Christ. Each one of us is a member with special gifts to share. Jesus's mission on earth was to call a community together and empower them for ministry in the world. Jesus said, "When I go, I will send my spirit, and my spirit will empower you. All things the Father told me, I'm telling you. All the things I'm doing, you will also do, even greater things than I" (see John 14–16).

The ministry of the body of Christ is not really something that you try to *do*, although it calls you to do many things. Ministry is the fruit of finding your gifts and offering what you have. Ministry is not something that requires professional credentials. It is a vocation each of us claims by virtue of our baptism in the body of Christ. Ministry isn't something you do for certain hours during the day and then you come home and relax at night. Well, who knows? Ministry might happen while you are relaxing.

If you are living in communion with God, if you know you are the beloved, and if you make yourself available for service, you cannot do other than minister. Ministry is the overflow of your love for God and others. *Ministry is when two people toast their glasses of wine and something splashes over.* Ministry is the extra.

MUTUALITY IN MINISTRY

"Serving others would be easier if I did not have to do it by myself," you may be saying. Or you may, like me, have the tendency to want to go from solitary communion to ministry without forming community. My individualism and desire for personal success over and again tempt me to do it alone and claim the task of ministry for myself. But Jesus did not preach or heal alone. Ministry is not meant to be done alone but in community. Ministry is not something we have and offer to another in need, but something offered and received in mutual vulnerability and benefit. Ministry is a communal and mutual experience. We don't minister *to;* we minister *with* and *among* others. "For where two or three meet in my name, I am there among them" (Matthew 18:20).

Jesus sent his followers out two by two to heal, drive out demons, and announce his coming (see Luke 9 and 10). We cannot bring good news on our own. We are called to proclaim the gospel together, in community. That's why I like to minister with others. I have found over and over how hard it is to be truly faithful to Jesus when I am alone. I need my brothers and sisters to pray with me, to speak with me about the spiritual task at hand, and to challenge me to stay pure in mind, heart, and body.

In my younger years, I traveled a lot, preaching and giving retreats as well as commencement and keynote addresses, and I always went alone. In my later years, I have gone out in ministry with people from the Daybreak community. They have special gifts that minister in ways that I cannot, and together, something special happens. For example, when Bill Van Buren and I were traveling together and speaking to large crowds, I was trying to say something that would make everybody listen. He was standing beside me. After I made the point, there was total silence. And then suddenly Bill blurted out: "Wow! I've heard this before!" In the spontaneity and laughter, something unexpected happened. He was a little needle in my balloon, but at the same time, we were together. People realized that it was not what I said that could make ministry happen. It was not what he said, but what *we* said and were together that was the good news. Indeed, whenever we minister together, it is easier for people to recognize that we do not come in our own name, but in the name of the Lord Jesus who sent us. When the community goes out together, ministry happens.

GRATITUDE AND COMPASSION

How can we cultivate a ministry community? Mutuality in ministry can be characterized by two words: *gratitude* and *compassion*. We minister together through paying attention to expressing our spirit of gratitude and our compassion for others. If you are looking for a community to belong to, look for these characteristics.

Gratitude basically means "to receive the gifts of God and others"—to say thank you. It is an essential part of ministry to recognize and receive the gifts of others and to say thank you to them for being who they are and for offering what they have. We have a desire to give things to people so that we can be on the giving side. We forget that the greater joy for other people is to realize that they have something to give to us. For example, I can care for handicapped people for the rest of my life, and they need a thousand things, but the greater joy is for them to be able to do some things for themselves and to offer their special gifts to others. When I take Bill or others from L'Arche on a lecture tour with me, it's not to show other people how much I care for them; rather, I do it so they can offer something and together with me share the good news.

Ministry is recognizing and receiving the gifts of others. I recognize in you a divine presence. You are the Christ who comes to me in the stranger, the prisoner, the one who is naked, who is hungry. It's not because of your needs, but because you have special gifts to share. Through you and your giving, I receive the gift of love and see the face of God. I am grateful. And I hope you recognize how beautiful you are!

One of the greatest temptations of life is to become resentful. *Resentment is the opposite of gratitude.* The world is full of resentment. What is resentment? Cold anger. Anger turned inward. We say, "I'm not angry at him. I'm angry at this. This is not the way I want it." Things do not turn out as expected, and we resent it. The older we get, the more chances we have to be resentful. I mean, what would we talk about if we had nothing about which to complain?

Ministry happens when we move from resentment to gratitude. The spiritual life is one of gratitude. Can you be grateful for everything that has happened in your life—not just for the good things but for all that has brought you to this day? Remember, it was the suffering of God's Son that brought forth a family of people known as Christians. My own suffering is what God used to bring me to where I am today.

Our ministry is to help people and let them help us gradually to let go of resentment and to discover that right in the middle of the pain there is a blessing for which we can be grateful. Right in the middle of the tears, the dance of joy can be felt. Seen from below, from a human perspective, there is an enormous distinction between good times and bad, between sorrow and joy. But from above, in the eyes of God, sorrow and joy are never separated. Where there is pain, there is also healing. Where there is mourning, there is dancing. Where there is poverty, there is the kingdom.

In ministry together, by our simple joy and grateful presence, we can help people become more grateful for life even with pain. Ministers, disciples of Jesus, go where there is pain, not because we are masochists, but because God is hidden in the pain and suffering of the world.

Compassion is the second word that makes service through ministry possible. Compassion means "to suffer with." In Latin, *com* means "with" and *passion* means "suffering." In the Old Testament, the principal words for God's compassion and ours are variations of the Hebrew word *rachamim*, which literally means "bowels," "womb,"or "gut." The corresponding Greek word for compassion in the New Testament is *splachmizomai*, which means "to be moved in the bowels, in the guts."[33] Compassion is visceral.

For example, when Jesus raised a widow's only son from the dead, he did so out of a broken heart of compassion:

> Jesus went to a town called Nain, and his disciples went along with him. As he approached the town gate, a dead person was being carried out—the only son of his mother, and she was a widow. And a large crowd from the town was with her. When the Lord saw her, *his heart went out to her,* and he said, "Don't cry." Then he went up and touched the coffin, and those carrying it stood still. He said, "Young man, I say to you, get up!" The dead man sat up and began to talk, and Jesus gave him back to his mother [emphasis added]. (Luke 7:11–15)

Jesus, moved with compassion, felt the pain of that mother in his guts. He felt it so deeply in his spirit that his compassion called her son back to life. Likewise, those who are moved with compassion "to suffer with those who suffer" witness to God's suffering presence and solidarity with those in need. God's name is *Emmanuel,* which means "God with us."

But what if we cannot solve the problems or change the circumstances of those we seek to help? Alleviating pain and suffering may sometimes be the fruit of our being with those who suffer, but that is not primarily why we are there. Ministry takes courage to be with the sick, the dying, and the poor in their weakness and in our powerlessness. We can't fix their problems or even answer their questions. We dare to be with others in mutual vulnerability and ministry precisely because God is a God who suffers with us and calls us to gratitude and compassion in the midst of pain. You cannot solve all the world's problems, but you can be with people in their problems and questions with your simple presence, trusting that joy also will be found there. As Mother Teresa was fond of saying, "Jesus does not call you to be successful, but to be faithful."

Jesus said, "Be compassionate as your heavenly Father is compassionate." It's a great calling. Don't be afraid. Don't say, "I can't do that." When you know yourself to be the beloved, and when you have friends around you with whom you live in community, you can do anything. You're not afraid anymore to knock on the door while someone is dying. You're not afraid to open a discussion with a person who beneath the glitter is much in need of ministry. Knowing that you are loved allows you to go into this world and touch people, heal them, speak with them, and make them aware that they are beloved, chosen, and blessed. Not by our might or by our power but by our simple presence in the midst of suffering, we show our love and gratitude for others. This is the mystery of ministry.

VOLUNTARY DISPLACEMENT AND DOWNWARD MOBILITY

Compassion and gratitude in ministry are possible through the twin disciplines of *downward mobility* and *voluntary displacement*. Together, they help us stay faithful to the calling to serve and minister to the poor.

Downward Mobility

The society in which we live suggests in countless ways that the way to go is up. Make it to the top, enter the limelight, break the record—that's what draws attention and gets us on the front page of the newspaper and offers the rewards of money and fame. Our culture values "upward mobility": staying on a secure career path, maintaining the status quo, appearing to others as an interesting person, succeeding in business, politics, sports, academics, or even spiritual practice.

The "world" (in the Johannine sense of *mundus*, literally, a "dark place") suggests to us, in thousands of ways, that we really should try to become a center of attention. We should strive to be distinct personalities standing out in the anonymous crowd. Our educational system nurtures this in us, and the media, as the messages come to us through newspapers, radio, and television, reinforce this. We are interesting when we do things other people do not do, say things other people do not say, and think things other people do not think. When we do, say, or think those things long enough and with enough publicity, we get medals, prizes, promotions, and commemorative plaques. The great seduction of the dark world is indeed being seduced into desiring to become an object of interest rather than a *subject* of compassion.

The way of Jesus is radically different than the spirit of the world. It is the way of *downward mobility*. It is going to the end of the line, staying behind the sets, and choosing the last place! Why is the way of Jesus worth choosing? Because it is the way to the kingdom and the way that brings life everlasting.

Everything in me wants to move upward. Downward mobility with Jesus goes radically against my inclinations, against the advice of the world surrounding me, and against the culture of which I am a part. In choosing to become poor with the poor of L'Arche, I still hope to gain praise for that choice. Wherever I turn I am confronted with my deep-seated resistance against following Jesus on his way to the Cross and my countless ways of avoiding poverty, whether material, intellectual, or emotional. Only Jesus, in whom the fullness of God dwells, could freely and fully choose to be completely poor and humble.

The great mystery of the Incarnation is how God descended to humanity and became one of us and, once among us, descended to the total dereliction of one condemned to death. At each critical moment of his journey, Jesus obediently chose the way downwards. In the first century of Christianity, there was already a hymn being sung about this descending way of Christ. Paul puts it into his Letter to the Philippians (2:5–8) in order to commend to his people the downward direction on the ladder of life. He writes:

> *Make your own mind the mind of Christ Jesus:*
> *Who, being in the form of God,*
> *did not count equality with God*

something to be grasped.
But emptied himself,
taking the form of a slave,
becoming as human beings are;
and being in every way like a human being,
he was humbler yet,
even to accepting death, death on a cross.

Here, expressed in summary but very plain terms, is the way of God's love. It is a way that goes down further and further into the greatest destitution: the destitution of a criminal whose life is taken from him. How is it possible for the descending way of Jesus to give rise to a new kind of community, grounded in love? It's very important that you come to understand this from the inside, so that a desire to follow Jesus in his descending way can gradually grow in you.

Voluntary Displacement

We are called to follow Jesus on the downward path of ministry and to go to where God is leading, even if that place is "somewhere we would rather not go" (John 21:18).

Following Jesus involves leaving the comfortable place and going to a place that is outside our comfort zone. Spiritual displacement is what is called for. The dictionary says that to *displace* is "to move or to shift from the ordinary or proper place." As a ship at sea displaces water, so are we displaced when something greater than ourselves moves us in a new direction or state of being. For displacement to be a real discipline, it has to be voluntary. Voluntary displacement prevents us from being caught in the net of the ordinary and proper. It is the discipline essential to remembering who we really are and remaining in touch with our greatest gifts of gratitude and compassion.

Voluntary displacement unmasks the illusion that we have to "make it to the top" and offers us a glimpse of a deeper spiritual reality. It puts us in touch with our own suffering and pain, our own woundedness and brokenness, our own limitations and powerlessness. As long as we want to be interesting, distinct, special, and worthy of special praise, we are pulled away from the deep realization that we are like other people, that we are part of the human race, and, in the final analysis, that we are not different but the same.

The discipline of displacement calls us away from the comfortable place and the easy oasis. To be called means to be always on the way, always moving, always searching, always hoping, always looking forward. Our vocation may require pursuit of a certain career. It may become visible in a concrete job or task. But it can never be reduced to this. It is not our career but our vocation that counts in the spiritual life. As soon as we begin to identify our career with our vocation, we are in danger of ending up in "an ordinary and proper place," unmindful of the fact that the wounds we still have are calling us to continue our search together with our fellow pilgrims.

For Thomas Merton, displacement meant leaving the university and going into a monastery. For Martin Luther, it meant leaving the monastery and becoming a reformer. For Dietrich Bonhoeffer, it meant returning to his country from the safety of the United States and becoming a prisoner of the Nazis. For Martin Luther King, Jr., it meant leaving the "ordinary and proper place" of blacks and leading a movement for civil rights. For Mother Teresa, it meant leaving the convent and starting an order to care for the "poorest of the poor" in Calcutta. For Jean Vanier, it meant leaving academia to live with the physically and mentally handicapped at L'Arche.

For many people, displacement means persevering faithfully in their unspectacular daily life, leaving grand fantasies aside to be faithful to their ministry in the marketplace. For others, it means leaving their jobs and security in a voluntary act of downward mobility in order to be free for ministry.

Many people do not have to displace themselves. They are displaced involuntarily. For them, the challenge is not moving out of "the ordinary and proper place" but making the given circumstances of their existence into a vocation. The question they have to answer is: How can I convert my forced displacement into something voluntary? But whatever displacement means in the concrete life of an individual person, it is a necessary prerequisite to ministry.

The remarkable paradox of displacement and downward mobility is that it creates community. When Francis of Assisi left his ordinary and proper place in society, tore off his clothes, and went off by himself to live in a cave, he laid bare not only his body but also the deep wounds in his own heart. His displacement became a witness to the basic human condition of brokenness and to the need for God's grace. Others were inspired to join him in his life of poverty. Soon, the Order of the Franciscans was born.

Often when someone voluntarily displaces himself or herself for the sake of the Kingdom, a prophetic community is formed. Sometimes it happens during their lives (Benedict, Francis, Ignatius, George Fox, John Wesley, Mother Teresa, Brother Roger). Sometimes it occurs after they die (Charles de Foucauld, Dietrich Bonhoeffer, Thomas Merton, Martin Luther King, Jr.). When displacement brings us in touch with our own wounded condition and allows us to become present to the suffering other, then community becomes the first place where the fruits of compassion are made visible.

When I stand in the presence of the Lord with empty hands, as a useless servant, I become aware of my basic dependence and my deep need for grace. Prayer helps me break down my pretense of wholeness and "self-fulfillment." It invites me to bend my knees, close my eyes, and stretch out my arms. In prayer, I hear God's voice calling me to move forward. I find my way home; I discover my vocation to care and be cared for in community.

Minister with Others

So how can you be of service? What is your ministry to others? Where are you to spend your time? Go to the place where people are in pain, but don't go alone. Go with others who have learned how to be grateful for the good and bad of life. Go with those who can sit with others in need, even if problems and pain persist. Let your heart be broken, and rely on Jesus's example of self-emptying so that you can be filled by God's strength. Then you will find the Messiah in your midst.

GOING DEEPER: EXERCISES FOR SPIRITUAL DIRECTION

I like to think of the spiritual life as the turning of a wagon wheel: when we run along the rim, we can reach only one spoke at a time, but when we start at the hub, we are in touch with all the spokes at once as well as the rim. What does the wheel represent? The hub is communion with God in our heart, connecting with the many spokes of community, on out to the rim of the wheel of ministry. If we are too active in our ministry, it's like we are running around the rim trying to reach everybody at once, all the time. But God says, "Start in the hub; live in the hub. Then you will be connected with all the spokes. And when you get to the rim, you won't have to run so fast."

Discuss some of the following questions with your spiritual director or community group:

In what ways are you trying to serve others from the "rim" of the wheel? What would happen if you began your ministry from the "hub" and included the "spokes" in offering service to others?

Currently, with whom are you in ministry? What is the value of going out "two by two" to serve and share the gospel?

If ministry is the "splash-over" of cups of joy filled to the brim, in what ways is your life filled and overflowing with love for others? In what ways is your ministry a drain on your spiritual life? How can you balance the wagon wheel of life and ministry?

Ask someone in your community: "What do you think are my gifts for ministry?" How does their answer compare with your own gift assessment?

After having taken this journey in spiritual direction, what will you do now? What spiritual disciplines or practices will you commit to in community? What promises will you make in order to fully live a spiritual life? Often in spiritual direction, individuals commit to a rule of life or a pattern of spiritual practices. As you reflect on your own journey, let me share with you the practices I committed to and promises I made after several years of soul-searching and after completing my first year at L'Arche Daybreak community, which had become my spiritual home.

On July 21, 1987, I celebrated the thirtieth anniversary of my ordination to the priesthood. Considering all that I had experienced during my first year at Daybreak, I didn't feel like having a party. Instead, I asked a few of the permanent members of the community to pray with me, reflect with me on my gifts and vocation, and offer me some critical guidance.

It was a painful experience for me in many ways. I had to face all my limitations and shortcomings directly, share them with my friends, and reach out to God and the community for help. But it was also a very life-giving experience. Seeing my handicaps so clearly, those surrounding me offered all their support, guidance, and love. This helped me make them not just stumbling blocks, but gateways to solidarity with those who cannot hide their disabilities and who form the core of our community.

During this anniversary celebration, I made three promises for the years to come and asked the community to help me be faithful to them. First of all, I promised to pray more. If, indeed, Jesus is the center of my life, I have to give him much more time and attention. I especially want to pray the prayer of adoration in which I focus on God's love, his compassion, and his mercy rather than on my needs, my problems, and my desires. Much of my prayer in the past has been introspective. I know that by moving from self-centered reflections to simple adoration I will come increasingly in touch with the reality of God and the reality of the people of God with whom I live.

Second, I promised to do everything possible to come to know my own community better. Many of the core community members and their assistants had remained strangers to me during that first year. The many invitations to do things outside of the community as well as my tendency to look for support in one or two friendships prevented me from making the whole of the community my true home. Having meals at different houses, "wasting time" with my own people, talking, playing, and praying with them, and allowing them to really know me, this requires a special discipline. It asks for a new way of scheduling my hours, for more "no's" to outside requests, and for the strong conviction that those with whom I live are my true family. Thus I will come to know Jesus not only in the solitude of prayer, but also in the community of love.

Finally, I promised to keep writing as part of my vocation and ministry. In the generally over-scheduled life of a community such as Daybreak, it is very hard to find the quiet hours necessary to write. Yet the call to Daybreak included the call to keep writing. Without writing I am not truly faithful to the ministry of the word that has been given to me. It is through writing that my hidden life with God and those with physical and mental disabilities can become a gift to the Church and the world. So, it is up to me to commit to the discipline of writing the words that emerge from my prayer life in community with handicapped persons and their assistants. Even though following Jesus might well become a more hidden journey, it should not ever become a private journey. For me, this means communicating as honestly as possible the pains and the joys, the darkness and the light, the fatigue and the vitality, the despair and the hope of going with Jesus to places where I would rather not go. By giving words to these intimate experiences, I can make my own life available to others and thus become a witness to the Word of Life whom "I have heard, seen

with my own eyes, watched and touched with my own hands"
(1 John 1:1).

I am glad to be surrounded by people who want to keep me
faithful to my promises, and to whom I wish to be accountable. It
is my prayer and hope that you too will commit to the practices
and disciplines of community life and spiritual direction. The
Spirit of God invites us to *look within to the heart, look to God in
the book*, and *look to others in community* in order to live the questions on the long walk of faith.

REFLECT AND JOURNAL:

*How might ministry and service happen when you are relax-
ing and enjoying yourself and others?*

Who in your community ministers with you and to you?

*What pain and suffering have you had to endure in your
life that brought you to the place where you are today?
We minister to each other when we ask and listen to the
answer to this question.*

*When you can't fix a problem, how can simply being present
to someone in pain or trouble help? Can you accept your
powerlessness in ministry?*

EPILOGUE:
Where Do I Go from Here?

Editors' note: Offering and receiving spiritual direction was a regular part of Henri's life. Reflection on the spiritual life was one of his core disciplines and the source of many of his books. Yet his vision of spiritual direction was not static. Beyond the foundations laid in the one article he wrote on the topic, his growing understanding is revealed in his notes, speeches, and journal entries during the final year of his life.

In Sabbatical Journey, written during his final months, Henri again articulates his lifelong struggle to find vocation, intimacy, and belonging. He also asks new questions about the spiritual life and seeks a new language to better express his experience of God on the long walk of faith. He also begins to speak about a fourth category of spiritual discipline. In addition to the three disciplines of the spiritual life he articulated earlier—the Heart, the Book, and the Church—a fourth discipline, the discipline of the body, can be discerned in the later Nouwen. The discipline of the body—the need to listen to the truth of the body and to "bring your body home"—challenged him to expand his notion of spiritual direction and formation and to move into a new spirituality of embodiment. Because he did not develop these thoughts systematically, we did not include this new direction in the book. But in this epilogue, we present the broad strokes of Henri's new spirituality-in-the-making. We also have clues that he was struggling to find the parable and live the questions of an embodied spirituality. He wanted to write a story that would simply speak for itself. He wanted to find a life that allowed human and divine, body and spirit, to catch hands and soar.

~The Flyer and the Catcher~

A Flyer and a Catcher enter the circus ring and greet the audience with smiles and movements that cause their wide silver capes to swirl about them. They pull themselves up into the large net and start to climb rope ladders to positions high up in the big tent. As the Flyer swings away from the pedestal board, she somersaults and turns freely in the air, only to be safely grasped by the Catcher.[34]

The Flying Rodleighs are trapeze artists who perform in the German circus Simoneit-Barum. When the circus came to Freiburg a few years ago, my friends invited me and my father to see the show. I will never forget how enraptured I became when I first saw the Rodleighs move through the air, flying and catching each other as elegant dancers. The next day I returned to the circus to see them again and introduced myself to them as one of their great fans. They invited me to attend their practice sessions, gave me free tickets, asked me to dinner, and suggested that I travel with them for a week through Germany.

I certainly was "hooked" by the Rodleighs and felt driven to see them perform again and again and to enter deeply into their world. One day I was sitting with Rodleigh, the leader of the troupe, in his caravan, talking about flying. He said, "As a flyer, I must have complete trust in my catcher. The public might think that I am the great star of the trapeze, but the real star is Joe, my catcher. He has to be there for me with split-second precision and grab me out of the air as I come to him in the long jump." "How does it work?" I asked. "The secret," Rodleigh said, "is that the flyer does nothing and the catcher does everything. When I fly to Joe, I have simply to stretch out my arms and hands and wait for him to catch me and pull me safely up."

"You do nothing!" I said, surprised.

"Nothing," Rodleigh repeated. "The worst thing the flyer can do is try to catch the catcher. I am not supposed to catch Joe. It's Joe's task to catch me. If I grab Joe's wrists, I might break them, or he might break mine, and that would be the end of both of us. A flyer must fly, and a catcher must catch, and the flyer must trust, with outstretched arms, that his catcher will be there for him."

What I heard from Rodleigh touched something very deep and intimate within me. It brought back yearnings I'd had as a seventeen-year-old boy for intimacy, relationship, and self-transcendence. Getting to know the Rodleighs captivated me and set me on a new journey toward a new image of my belovedness. Real spiritual life, I became aware, is an enfleshed life calling for a new spirituality of the body. To believe in the Incarnation—that God becomes flesh—is to realize that God enters into the body, so that if you touch a body, in a way you touch the divine life. There is no divine life outside the body because God decided to become one of us.

There is so much more to say about embodied spirituality and the discipline of the body, but I do not yet have the words; I have only questions and a new direction. Yet, deep within myself, I feel that something new wants to be born: a book with stories, a novel, a spiritual embodiment journal—something quite different from what I have done in the past. To write about my experience with the Rodleighs would require a radical new step in my life, one I'm not quite ready to take.

Over the years I have built up a certain reputation. People think of me as a Catholic priest, a spiritual writer, a member of a community with mentally handicapped people, a lover of God, and a lover of people. It is wonderful to have such a reputation. But lately I find I get caught in it and I experience it as restricting. Without wanting to, I feel a certain pressure within me to keep living up to that reputation and to do, say, and write things that fit the expectations of the Catholic Church, L'Arche, my family, my friends, my readers. I'm caught because I'm feeling that there is some kind of agenda I must follow in order to be faithful.

New thoughts, feelings, emotions, and passions have arisen within me that are not all in line with my previous thoughts and feelings. So I find myself asking, What is my responsibility to the world around me, and what is my responsibility to myself? What does it mean to be faithful to my vocation? Does it require that I be consistent with my earlier way of living or thinking, or does it ask for the courage to move in new directions, even when doing so may be disappointing for some people?

I remind myself that Jesus died when he was in his early thirties. How would Jesus have lived and thought if he had lived into his sixties? Would he have disappointed his followers? I don't know. But for me, many new questions and concerns emerge at my present age that weren't there in the past. For example, what to do with my life between ages sixty and eighty? How should I relate to those who do not live or believe as I do? What is the place of gay persons in the Church, evangelical Christians in the world, and people committed to other religions in eternity? The more I travel and meet other people whose vision of the spiritual life differs from mine, the more I learn and grow.

I am also surprised that some of the fundamental questions I thought I had answered earlier in my life re-present themselves to me in my sixties: Who am I? What is my vocation? How can I bring my body home? How best to deal with my need for intimacy and affection as a celibate priest?

Because what is most personal is most universal, I know you ask some of the same questions and struggle with similar issues of life. Questions of identity, purpose, calling, community, and ministry continue to surface with new urgency at different seasons of our lives. Issues of intimacy and sexuality, aging and embodiment, are common to the spiritual life. I urge you, as I remind myself, to live the questions deeply, knowing that you and I are God's beloved.

As I continue to pray and write and be faithful to God and to the community I serve, I want to be free enough to live the questions of the spiritual life without fearing the consequences. I know that I am not completely free, because the fear is still there. I know that to reach a new integration of solitude, intimacy, and creativity is far ahead of me. In the meantime, there are three things that are most important to me now: living a vision inspired by the gospel of Jesus; being close to the poor, the handicapped, the sick, and the dying; and finding a way to satisfy the deep yearning for intimacy, affection, and self-transcendence that resurfaced in me in my friendship with the Flying Rodleighs.

As I watch the Rodleighs flying and catching under the big top, I find myself crying. The choreography is elegant, there are many wonderful surprises, and the whole performance feels very energetic. How intimate is the circus tent. Even though I have seen the Flying Rodleighs for five years and have attended dozens of their shows, they never bore me. There is always something new, something original, something fresh. As I watch them in the air, I feel some of the same profound emotion as when I saw them for the first time with my father in 1991. It is hard to describe, but it is the emotion coming from an experience of enfleshed spirituality—body and spirit fully united. The body in its beauty and elegance expresses the spirit of love, friendship, and community, and the spirit never leaves the here and now of the body. I want to live trusting the catcher.

APPENDIX ONE
Living the Questions:
Ten Parables of Henri Nouwen

QUESTION	PARABLE*
Who will answer my questions?	"The Zen Master" (3)
Where do I begin?	"The Lion in the Marble" (16)
Who am I?	"The Fugitive and the Rabbi" (26)
Where have I been and where am I going?	"God's Story of Adam" (39)
What is prayer?	"Three Monks on an Island" (55)
Who is God for me?	"Four Blind Men and the Elephant" (71)
How do I hear the word?	"Word and Wisdom" (86)
Where do I belong?	"Darkness and the Dawn" (109)
How can I be of service?	"Where to Find the Messiah?'" (128)
Where do I go from here?	"The Flyer and the Catcher" (148)

Numbers in parentheses indicate page number on which each parable appears.

APPENDIX TWO
How to Find a Spiritual Director
by Rebecca J. Laird

Finding a spiritual director begins with prayer. Most people begin by looking at a directory, calling a local retreat center, or asking ministers and priests for referrals. Those steps are necessary and useful, but the true place to start is to invite God to do the leading. Perhaps my story will give you clues on how to begin.

When I first learned in a seminary course on the history of Christian spirituality about a "spiritual director," I knew immediately that I needed to find one. I was in my midtwenties, facing personal struggles and trying to sort out my own vocational call. I was a Protestant student taking classes in a Catholic seminary to fill in the blanks I had about the Christian spiritual tradition before the Reformation, and I had no idea how to start looking. I had noticed a United Methodist clergywoman in my classes who showed wisdom in her questions, so I timidly asked her to have coffee with me after class.

As we talked, this wise soul, whose name was Barbara, revealed that she was trained in spiritual direction but was on sabbatical. She would be willing, however, to suggest someone. To become more familiar with me, she asked some questions: "What draws you to spiritual direction? What kind of qualities in a person put you at ease to share your spiritual life? Tell me a bit about your spiritual journey and how you got to where you are today. Where do you live, and how often are you able to set aside the time for spiritual direction?" We prayed for God to guide her as she considered her contacts and for God to grant me an open heart toward the one to whom God would lead me. We arranged to meet again the next week after class.

All week I prayed to be open, but Barbara's own face kept coming into view as I took time to ask for God's leading. I suspected, since I knew no one else who offered spiritual direction, that I was simply suggestible. But the pull persisted. When we met the next week, I was nervous. I didn't know how to say aloud that I wanted her to be my spiritual director. I knew she was on sabbatical and rightly guarding her time. As God would have it, I didn't have to muster the courage. She looked at me and said, with a mystified look on her face, "I looked through my list of colleagues, but I sensed God's nudge for me to offer myself as a director for you." I nearly wept with gratitude. She cleared space and time for me, and we began a relationship of spiritual direction. She told me this was a gift she was choosing to give to me as others had freely given to her. There was no financial charge.

For several years she welcomed me into her office. We explored life questions, of course. Since I was in my twenties, issues of sexuality, intimacy, and self-agency were never far from sight. I wouldn't have been able to see this at the time, but looking back, I recall working primarily on the questions: "Who am I?" and "To whom do I belong?"

Always a candle was lit; a teapot under a quilted tea cozy was hot and ready to pour. Barbara listened, prodded, challenged, loved, and prayed for and with me. She taught me to sit in silence. She asked me often about the quality, quantity, and substance of my prayers. Such a gift. When she told me she was moving, I felt like a fledgling ready to test my wings but knew I would miss her kindness and friendship, and I did.

A few years later a faith crisis initiated by a terrible crime forced me back into spiritual direction. This time I simply landed on the doorstep of a retreat center; an hour from home, it was a place I had frequented for personal retreats. The sister in charge of spiritual direction interviewed me and made a match. I followed her advice and met with Meg, a trained Catholic laywoman, at a location closer to my home. She didn't have a set fee, but I was asked to donate toward the rental space she used and to make any additional donation I wished. The church where we met kept an open account for her. She never knew who gave how much. It was a matter of faith, but she made it clear that some monetary exchange was essential.

Meg blew in at the last moment for appointments. She forgot matches for the candles. She could laugh uproariously with delight at the antics of life. She had to sometimes cancel or reschedule, as did I, but how well she understood the terrain of the soul. She mirrored back what she heard and linked my life with the great story of scripture. She was great at exploring dreams. When tears sprang to my eyes and I wanted to talk through the pain, she made me sit without words and simply feel the pain. She served as a guardian to my spirit as I learned to experience God in the chaos and clutter of my fears. Surely, God started to heal me and speak anew to me through Meg. We focused a lot on the life question: "Who is God for me?" The God I understood from childhood no longer seemed viable in the face of great violence. I had to expand my view of God; my old version was too small.

This time I was the one to move away and end our direction relationship. How I missed Meg when I moved across the country. My soul was stable in God, but how I missed one of the companions of my soul country.

Many years of caring for my small children ensued. I did not have the freedom or time or energy to meet regularly with anyone. I was new to my area and also didn't know where to begin. One day while talking with Gary, a friend from church, he said he wanted to start a prayer group. We came up with a group of eight people to invite to the group. Gary and Lisa, Jeff and Julie, John and Sally, and Michael and I agreed to meet monthly. What transpired, we came to understand, was group spiritual direction. We opened our hearts through a song, scripture, or inspirational reading, then one by one we spoke our souls; those who wanted to respond did so. We walked each other through childbirth, cancer, marital strife, graduations, and financial gains and losses, and we witnessed to the work of the Holy Spirit in each other's lives. Over years and moves, our group has morphed into a sturdy friendship. We no longer all live nearby, but we regularly reunite for fun and the deep enjoyment that lasts among spiritual friends.

Recently I returned to formal direction. After living in the East for years, I now know where the spiritual resources and retreat centers are located. I called one and was matched with an Episcopalian sister. I put my donation check to support the retreat center in a little wooden box. Direction this time is less structured, and I find at this time of life that my need for direction and what I receive from my director are less about my relationship with her and more about my reflections on my spiritual life before our meetings. After our meetings I try to stay to walk the labyrinth and pray as I walk about where I am in the journey of faith.

Knowing that someone will ask me about my spiritual life and not let me cruise or stay on the level of intention steadies me. When I drive to the cloistered grounds, every fiber of my being seems to know that this is soul time. Nothing else intrudes for a time. My soul sighs with relief no matter what is going on in my life.

For the past dozen years, I have also spent many hours in the spiritual director's chair. For me, there is no greater joy. After finishing seminary, I enrolled in a certification program in spiritual direction, and as if by some divine cue, people, mostly those struggling with vocational calls to ministry, began to seek me out.

Each time I get a call asking about spiritual direction, I arrange a first date to clarify expectations and get acquainted. I ask all who come to pray about the matter for at least a week. Several times I have clearly sensed that the inquirer and I should not proceed. Other times the week of prayer led the inquirer to look elsewhere. In these cases, I have recommended the person to someone else with a prayer of blessing. When God clearly makes a match for God's good reasons, we arrange to meet regularly for a few months and then reevaluate. Typically, I meet with only one or two persons regularly, and most relationships last for two to three years. Most come to my office once or twice a month. Emails sometimes are exchanged. One young woman asked for email direction, which we supplemented with long phone calls. Another came a long distance quarterly, and we wrote letters between visits. The mode differs, but the focus is on seeking God's activity in the midst of life questions. Practicing spiritual disciplines—journaling, reading scripture, seeking God in community, service, and daily prayer—and accepting spiritual accountability form the bedrock of the relationship.

So are you looking for a spiritual director? Begin with prayer. Follow that with conversations with clergy or religious leaders in your area. Listings of local retreat centers and a regional clearinghouse of spiritual directors is available online through Spiritual Direction International at www.sdiworld.org. Online spiritual directors who are available via email and phone calls and are connected with the work of Henri Nouwen are listed at the Henri Nouwen Society: www.henrinouwen.org.

Trust that God will lead you. After all, it is God's Spirit that does the guiding and real directing; the director is simply there to be God's friend and yours in the process.

For Further Reading

BOOKS BY HENRI J. M. NOUWEN

Adam: God's Beloved (Orbis, 1997)

Aging: The Fulfillment of Life (Doubleday, 1974)

Behold the Beauty of the Lord: Praying with Icons (Ave Maria Press, 1987)

Beyond the Mirror: Reflections on Death and Life (Crossroad, 1990)

Bread for the Journey: A Daybook of Wisdom and Faith (HarperCollins, 1997)

Can You Drink the Cup? The Challenge of the Spiritual Life (Ave Maria Press, 1996)

Clowning in Rome: Reflections on Solitude, Celibacy, Prayer, and Contemplation (Doubleday, 1979)

Compassion: A Reflection on the Christian Life (Doubleday, 1982)

Creative Ministry: Beyond Professionalism in Teaching, Preaching, Counseling, Organizing, and Celebrating (Doubleday, 1971)

A Cry for Mercy: Prayers from the Genesee (Doubleday, 1981)

Encounters with Merton (Crossroad, 2004)

Finding My Way Home: Pathways to Life and the Spirit, edited and with a preface by Sue Mosteller (Crossroad, 2001)

The Genesee Diary: Report from a Trappist Monastery (Doubleday, 1976)

Gracias! A Latin American Journal (Harper & Row, 1983)

Heart Speaks to Heart: Three Prayers to Jesus (Ave Maria Press, 1989)

Here and Now: Living in the Spirit (Crossroad, 1995)

In Memoriam (Ave Maria Press, 1980)

The Inner Voice of Love: A Journey Through Anguish to Freedom (Doubleday, 1996)

In the Name of Jesus: Reflections on Christian Leadership (Crossroad, 1989)

Intimacy: Pastoral Psychological Essays (Fides Publishers, 1969)

Jesus and Mary: Finding Our Sacred Center (Saint Anthony Messenger Press and Franciscan, 1993)

A Letter of Consolation (Harper & Row, 1982)

Letters to Marc About Jesus (HarperCollins, 1988)
Life of the Beloved: Spiritual Living in a Secular World (Crossroad, 1992)
Lifesigns: Intimacy, Fecundity, and Ecstasy in Christian Perspective
    (Doubleday, 1986)
The Living Reminder: Service and Prayer in Memory of Jesus Christ
    (Seabury, 1977)
Love in a Fearful Land: A Guatemalan Story (Orbis, 2006)
Making All Things New: An Invitation to the Spiritual Life (HarperCollins, 1981)
Ministry and Spirituality: Three Books in One (Continuum, 1996)
Our Greatest Gift: A Meditation on Dying and Caring (HarperCollins, 1994)
Out of Solitude: Three Meditations on the Christian Life (Ave Maria Press, 1974)
The Path of Waiting, The Path of Freedom, The Path of Power, and *The Path of*
    Peace (Crossroad, 1995)
Peacework: Prayer Resistance Community (Orbis, 2005)
Reaching Out: The Three Movements of the Spiritual Life (Doubleday, 1975)
The Return of the Prodigal Son (Doubleday, 1992)
The Road to Daybreak: A Spiritual Journey (Doubleday, 1988)
Sabbatical Journey: The Final Year (Crossroad, 1997)
Show Me the Way (Crossroad, 1994)
Spiritual Journals: Three Books in One (Continuum, 1997)
Walk with Jesus: Stations of the Cross (Orbis, 1990)
The Way of the Heart: Desert Spirituality and Contemporary Ministry
    (Seabury, 1981)
With Burning Hearts: A Meditation on the Eucharistic Life (Orbis, 1994)
With Open Hands (Ave Maria Press, 1972)
The Wounded Healer: Ministry in Contemporary Society (Doubleday, 1972)

SELECTED COMPILATIONS AND EDITED VOLUMES
BY AND ABOUT HENRI J. M. NOUWEN

Ford, Michael, ed., *Eternal Seasons: A Liturgical Journey with Henri J. M. Nou-*
    wen (Sorin Books/Darton, Longman & Todd, 2004)
Ford, Michael, ed., *The Wounded Prophet: A Portrait of Henri J. M. Nouwen*
    (Doubleday, 1999)
Greer, Wendy Wilson, ed. and comp., *The Only Necessary Thing: Living a*
    Prayerful Life: Selected Writings of Henri J. M. Nouwen (Crossroad, 1999)
Imbach, Jeff, ed., *Words of Hope and Healing: 99 Sayings* (New City Press, 2005)
Jonas, Robert A., ed., *Henri Nouwen: Writings* (Orbis Books, 1998)
Jones, Timothy, ed. and comp., *Turn My Mourning into Dancing: Finding Hope*
    in Hard Times (W Publishing Group/Thomas Nelson, 2001)

Laird, Rebecca, and Michael J. Christensen, eds., *The Heart of Henri Nouwen: His Words of Blessing* (Crossroad, 2003)
LaNoue, Deirdre, *The Spiritual Legacy of Henri Nouwen* (Continuum, 2000)
Mosteller, Sue, ed., *Finding My Way Home: Pathways to Life and the Spirit* (Crossroad, 2001)
O'Laughlin, Michael, *God's Beloved: A Spiritual Biography* (Orbis, 2004)
O'Laughlin, Michael, ed. *Jesus: A Gospel* by Henri J. M. Nouwen (Orbis, 2004)
———, *Henri Nouwen: His Life and Vision* (Orbis, 2005)
Porter, Beth, ed., with Susan M. S. Brown and Philip Coulter, *Befriending Life: Encounters with Henri Nouwen* (Doubleday, 2001)

BOOKS ON SPIRITUAL DIRECTION RECOMMENDED BY HENRI NOUWEN

Aelred of Rievaulx, *Spiritual Friendship* (Cistercian, 2005)
Anonymous, *The Way of a Pilgrim*, translated by Helen Bacovcin (Image, 1978)
Caussade, Jean-Pierre de, *The Sacrament of the Present Moment* (HarperSan-Francisco, 1989)
DeMello, Anthony, *Sadhana: A Way to God: Christian Exercises in Eastern Form* (Image, 1984)
Doyle, Charles, *Guidance in Spiritual Direction* (Mercer Press, 1958)
Edwards, Tilden, *Spiritual Friend: Reclaiming the Gift of Spiritual Direction* (Paulist Press, 1980)
Foster, Richard, *Celebration of Discipline: The Path to Spiritual Growth* (Harper & Row, 1978)
Isabell, Damien, *The Spiritual Director: A Practical Guide* (Franciscan Hearld Press, 1975)
Laplace, Jean, *Preparing for Spiritual Direction* (Franciscan Hearld Press, 1975)
Leech, Kenneth, *Soul Friend: A Study of Spirituality* (Sheldon Press, 1977)
Merton, Thomas, *Spiritual Direction and Meditation* (Liturgical Press, 1960)
———, *The Wisdom of the Desert: Sayings from the Desert Fathers of the Fourth Century* (Shambhala, 2004)
Mottola, Anthony, trans., *The Spiritual Exercises of St. Ignatius* (Doubleday, 1964)
Rahner, Karl, *Spiritual Exercises* (Herder and Herder, 1965)
Schneiders, Sandra M., *Spiritual Direction: Reflections on a Contemporary Ministry* (National Sisters Vocational Conference, 1977)
Steindl-Rast, Brother David, *Gratefulness, the Heart of Prayer: An Approach to Life in Fullness* (Paulist Press, 1984)
Teresa of Avila, *The Way of Perfection* (Image, 1991)

Van Kaam, Adrian, *The Dynamics of Spiritual Self-Direction* (Dimension Books, 1976)

Wright, Wendy M. and Joseph F. Power, comps., *Frances de Sales, Jane de Chantal: Letters of Spiritual Direction*, translated by Peronne Marie Thibert and with a foreword by Henri J. M. Nouwen (Paulist Press, 1988)

BOOKS ON THE SPIRITUAL LIFE RECOMMENDED BY HENRI NOUWEN

Athanasius, *The Life of St. Anthony*, translated by Robert Meyer, *Ancient Christian Writers*, vol. 10 (Newman Press, 1978)

Bloom, Anthony, *Beginning to Pray* (Paulist Press, 1970)

Bonhoeffer, Dietrich, *Life Together* (Harper & Row, 1954)

Bouyer, Louis, *A History of Christian Spirituality*, 3 vols. (Seabury Press, 1969)

Chariton of Valamo, Igumen, comp., *The Art of Prayer: An Orthodox Anthology* (Faber and Faber, 1966)

Eckhart, Meister, *Treatises on the Love of God* (Harper & Row, 1968)

Fox, Matthew, *On Becoming a Musical Mystical Bear: Spirituality American Style* (Paulist Press, 1972)

———, *Western Spirituality* (Claretian, 1979)

Hueck Doherty, Catherine de, *Poustinia: Christian Spirituality of the East for Western Man* (Ave Maria Press, 1975)

St. John of the Cross, *The Ascent of Mount Carmel* (Paraclete Press, 2002)

———, *Dark Night of the Soul*, translated by Mirabai Starr (Riverhead, 2003)

Johnston, William, *The Mysticism of the Cloud of Unknowing*, with a foreword by Thomas Merton (Desclee, 1967)

Julian of Norwich, *The Revelations of Divine Love*, translated by Elizabeth Spearing, with an introduction and notes by A. C. Spearing (Penguin, 1999)

Kadloubovsky, E., trans., *Early Fathers from the Philokalia* (Faber and Faber, 1954)

Kadloubovsky, E., and G. E. H. Palmer, trans., *Writings from the Philokalia: On Prayer of the Heart* (Faber and Faber, 1992)

Brother Lawrence, *The Practice of the Presence of God* (Revell, 1885)

Maloney, George, *Breath of the Mystic* (Dimension Books, 1974)

McNeill, John, *A History of the Cure of Souls* (Harper & Row, 1951)

Merton, Thomas, *Contemplative Prayer* (Herder and Herder, 1969)

———, *Contemplation in a World of Action* (Doubleday, 1971)

Pennington, Basil, *Daily We Touch Him* (Doubleday, 1977)

Teilhard de Chardin, Pierre, *Hymn of the Universe* (Harper & Row, 1963)

Ward, Benedicta, tr., *The Sayings of the Desert Fathers* (Mowbray & Co., 1975)

Ware, Kallilstos, *The Orthodox Way* (St. Vladimir's Seminary Press, 1995)

Wolff, Pierre, *May I Hate God?* (Paulist Press, 1979)

Notes

1. See "To Supervising Ministers" (Berkeley Divinity School Center, 1977).
2. See "Spiritual Direction" (*Reflection*, Yale Divinity School, 1981). Henri recommended—and assigned as required reading for his courses—*Spiritual Direction and Meditation* by Thomas Merton (Liturgical Press, 1960) and *Soul Friend* by Kenneth Leech (Sheldon Press, 1977).
3. *Making All Things New*, p. 69.
4. Other classical spiritual disciplines are subsumed under Nouwen's three disciplines: including poverty or simplicity, chastity, obedience, stability, fasting, meditation, contemplation, sacred reading, community, service, generosity, and many forms of interior prayer. See Richard Foster's *Celebration of Discipline* (Harper & Row, 1978).
5. Nouwen consistently used the word "heart" to mean our access point to God through contemplative, listening prayer and active obedience.
6. See Chapter Seven, "How Do I Hear the Word?", for further instruction on *lectio divina*.
7. Cited in "Living the Questions: The Spirituality of the Religion Teacher" (*Union Seminary Quarterly Review*, Fall 1976).
8. Likewise, the first task in spiritual direction is not to offer information, advice, or even guidance, but to allow people to come in touch with their own struggles, pains, doubts, and insecurities—in short, to affirm their life as a quest. See Todd Brennan's article and interview "A Visit with Henri Nouwen" (*The Critic* 36, no. 4, Summer 1978: 42–49).
9. Rainer Maria Rilke, *Letters to a Young Poet*, translated by M. D. Herter (Norton, 1954), pp. 46–47.
10. Ibid., pp. 34–35.

11. Henri provided these instructions for journal-keeping to his classes on spiritual direction and formation at Yale and Harvard. His *Genesee Diary* (1976) is an example of how he kept a journal for formation. Recommended journal-keeping resources include Ira Progoff, *At a Journal Workshop*, on how to write a journal and how to organize and structure it; and *Ariadne's Thread*, edited by Lyn Lifshin, a collection of excerpts from women's journals in which they offer their thoughts on what it means to keep a journal and how they do it.

12. Nouwen's story of the sculptor and the lion was inspired by Thomas Hora, *Existential Metapsychiatry* (Seabury Press, 1977); he uses it to illustrate the roles of the spiritual disciplines in "Spiritual Formation in Theological Education" (unpublished manuscript series, 1970–78) and in *Clowning in Rome* (1979), p. 86.

13. Cited by Nouwen first in "Generation Without Fathers," *Commonweal* 92 (June 1970): 287–94, and then in *The Wounded Healer* (1972), pp. 25–26.

14. Arthur LeClair, "The Beloved Prayer," *Sacred Journey* (December 1996): 21–23.

15. *L'Arche* means "Noah's Ark" in French and is the name of an international network of communities of persons with disabilities and their assistants and caregivers. From 1986 to 1996, Henri lived at Daybreak, a L'Arche community in Richmond Hills, Ontario, where he was Adam's assistant. His book *Adam: God's Beloved* (1996) contains the full story.

16. "God's Story of Adam," unpublished prologue to *Adam: God's Beloved* (Orbis Books, 1996).

17. Henri died on September 21, 1996, of a massive heart attack when he was visiting the Netherlands on his way to St. Petersburg to film a documentary on Rembrandt's *Return of the Prodigal Son*.

18. Tolstoy's parable is cited by Nouwen in *The Road to Daybreak: A Spiritual Journey* (1988), p. 50.

19. See R. M. French, trans., *The Way of a Pilgrim* (Seabury Press, 1965).

20. Pierre Wolff, *May I Hate God?* (Paulist Press, 1979).

21. *Psalms: A New Translation: Singing Version*, Joseph Gelineau, trans. (Paulist Press, 1966) Note the different numbering in this translation. Other versions are numbered one greater (e.g., 116=117).

22. Ibid.

23. Adapted from the *Buddhist Sutra*.

24. Psalm 90 from *Psalms: A New Translation: Singing Version*.

25. Anonymous, *The Cloud of Unknowing*.

26. Dietrich Bonhoeffer, *Letters and Papers from Prison*, edited by Eberhard Bethge (Macmillan, 1972), p. 360, cited by Nouwen in *The Living Reminder* (1977).

27. "Be Still and Know" was presented by Henri as part of an Advent meditation series at Yale Divinity School on November 7, 1979.

28. Yushi Nomura, *Desert Wisdom* (Doubleday, 1982), pp. 14, 38–39.

29. Thomas Merton, *The Way of Chuang Tzu* (New Directions, 1965), p. 154, used by Henri in "Unceasing Prayer," *America* (July 1978).

30. Whether this exercise of centering prayer was originally written by Nouwen or appropriated from someone else, Nouwen made use of it in class and shared it in a published article "Centering Prayer" (*Centering*, 4(1), 1987).

31. Although Henri told this parable many times, it most recently appears in *Finding My Way Home* (2001), p. 87.

32. Cited by Henri from the tractate Sanhedrin in *The Wounded Healer: Ministry in Contemporary Society* (1972), ch. 4.

33. In class Henri explained the roots of compassion by referring to the biblical research done by his teaching assistant John Mogabgab in a handout entitled "Compassion: Selected Biblical References." See also Henri's book *Compassion: A Reflection on the Christian Life* (1982).

34. Adapted from Nouwen's telling of the story in a transcript of "Our Story, Our Wisdom" (recorded at Loyola University, 1994), reprinted in *Our Greatest Gift* (1994).

Primary Sources and Notations

INTRODUCTION: SPIRITUAL DIRECTION
"Spiritual Direction" (*Reflections*, Yale Divinity School, 1981) is Nouwen's only
   published article on the subject. It later was reprinted in *Worship* (1981) and
   The Word (1982) and excerpted in *Henri Nouwen: In My Own Words*, edited
   by Robert Durback (2001). This integrated and edited version provides the
   core material for this introduction and for the structure of the book as a
   whole.
"Moving from Solitude to Community and Ministry," *Leadership* (Spring 1995).
"Parting Words: An Interview with Rebecca Laird," *Sacred Journey* (September 1996).
Excerpts from *Clowning in Rome: Reflections on Solitude, Celibacy, Prayer, and
   Contemplation* (1979), *Life of the Beloved: Spiritual Living in a Secular World*
   (1992), *Making All Things New: An Invitation to the Spiritual Life* (1981), and
   Letters to Marc About Jesus (1988).

CHAPTER 1: WHO WILL ANSWER MY QUESTIONS?
The core of this chapter is an edited version of "Living the Questions: The
   Spirituality of the Religion Teacher," *Union Seminary Quarterly Review*
   (Fall 1976). Additional material is added and adapted from the unpublished
   version of "Spiritual Formation in Theological Education" (1978 or 1979).
   Additional excerpts are adapted from *Here and Now: Living in the Spirit* (1995)
   and *Reaching Out: The Three Movements of the Spiritual Life* (1975).

CHAPTER TWO: WHERE DO I BEGIN?
The core content of this chapter is adapted from "Spiritual Direction" (*Reflection*, Yale Divinity School, 1981) and Todd Brennan's article and interview
   "A Visit with Henri Nouwen," *The Critic* (Summer 1978).

Additional excerpts are adapted from *Reaching Out* (1975) and *Clowning in Rome* (1979).

CHAPTER THREE: WHO AM I?

The core content of this chapter is consolidated and adapted from "Parting Words" (1996) and from "Being the Beloved," a sermon preached by Henri at the Crystal Cathedral, for the *Hour of Power* television program, August 23, 1992, and published in *Henri Nouwen: Writings*, edited by Robert A. Jonas (1998). The content is published in its fullest and most polished form in *Life of the Beloved* (1992).

Additional excerpts are adapted from "Generation Without Fathers," *Commonweal* (June 1970) and *Reaching Out* (1975).

CHAPTER FOUR: WHERE HAVE I BEEN AND WHERE AM I GOING?

"God's Story of Adam" is Nouwen's unpublished prologue to his published book *Adam: God's Beloved* (1996). In publishing it here for the first time, we hope to illustrate Henri's conviction that we are loved with an everlasting love before our birth and after our death. We are grateful to Virginia Hall Birch, who typed the original manuscript of *Adam* for Henri, and to the Henri Nouwen Literary Trust for permission to include "God's Story of Adam" in this chapter. "Two Voices" and "My Life with Adam" are adapted from "Finding Vocation in Downward Mobility," *Leadership* 11, no. 3 (Summer 1990): 60–61.

"My History with God" and "Guidelines for Presenting Our Sacred History" are unpublished course materials prepared by Henri for a class he taught at Regis College in Toronto (in 1994) and at L'Arche Daybreak in 1990. Excerpts from "My History with God" were included in *Road to Peace*, edited by John Dear, S.J. (1998).

Additional excerpts are taken from *Finding My Way Home: Pathways to Life and the Spirit*, edited by Sue Mosteller (2001).

CHAPTER FIVE: WHAT IS PRAYER?

The core of this chapter is adapted from *Clowning in Rome* (1979). Additional excerpts are incorporated from similar sources, including:

Nouwen's foreword to Pierre Wolff's *May I Hate God?* (Paulist Press, 1979).

"Prayer as Listening," lecture delivered at "A Conference on Prayer," Woodland Park Community of Celebration, June 23, 1980.

"Prayer and Ministry" (interview), *Sisters Today* 48, no. 6 (February 1977).

"Unceasing Prayer," *America* (July 1978).

"Prayer and Health Care," a sound recording of Nouwen's address to the 75th
Annual Catholic Health Assembly between June 10–13, 1990, in Washing-
ton, D.C. Catholic Health Assembly catalogue number CHA-603.
The prayer that ends the chapter is from *A Cry for Mercy: Prayers from the
Genesee* (1981).

CHAPTER SIX: WHO IS GOD FOR ME?

Nouwen's conversation with Abbot John Eudes Bamberger is recorded in the
entry for August 12, 1974, in *The Genesee Diary* (1976).
"God Is with Us" is adapted from *Compassion: A Reflection on the Christian Life*
(Doubleday, 1982).
"God Is Personal" is adapted from *The Return of the Prodigal Son* (1992). Nouwen also writes about the personal "fatherhood" and "motherhood" of God
in "The Vulnerable God," *Weavings* (July–August 1993), and in the June 11
and 12 entries in *Bread for the Journey: A Daybook of Wisdom and Faith* (1997).
Nouwen writes about the hiddenness of God and the mystery of God's
absence and presence primarily in *Creative Ministry: Beyond Professionalism
in Teaching, Preaching, Counseling, Organizing, and Celebrating* (1971) and in
Reaching Out (1975) and *Clowning in Rome* (1979).
Additional excerpts are taken from *The Living Reminder: Service and Prayer in
Memory of Jesus Christ* (1977), *Clowning in Rome* (1979), *Making All Things
New* (1981), and *The Genesee Diary* (1976).
"God is Looking for Us" is adapted from *Return of the Prodigal Son* (1992).
Henri presented the guided meditation "Be Still and Know" as part of an
Advent mediation series at Yale Divinity School on November 7, 1979.
The closing prayer is from April 15 in *A Cry for Mercy* (1981).

CHAPTER SEVEN: HOW DO I HEAR THE WORD?

The three quotations on the variant meanings of *word* are from Yushi Nomura, *Desert Wisdom* (Doubleday, 1982), pp. 14, 38, 39, for which Nouwen
wrote the introduction.
Much of the material in this chapter is consolidated and adapted from
unpublished sources, including "Intro to the Spiritual Life" (Harvard
lecture notes, 1985), "Theology as Doxology," and "Spiritual Formation in
Theological Education," (ca 1970–78). "Theology as Doxology" was eventually published as Chapter 5 in *Caring for the Commonweal: Education for
Religious and Public Life*, edited by Parker J. Palmer, Barbara G. Wheeler,
and James W. Fowler (1990).
Excerpts from the following published works are adapted and incorporated into
this chapter: *The Way of the Heart: Desert Spirituality and Contemporary Min-*

istry (1981), *Reaching Out* (1975), *Making All Things New* (1981), *With Burning Hearts: A Meditation on the Eucharistic Life* (1994), "Spiritual Direction" (1981), *Letters to Marc About Jesus* (1988), and *Bread for the Journey* (1997).

The story of the letter to the soldier is from Henri's sermon entitled "Renewed in the Spirit of Your Mind," Short Collected Sermons and Meditations, 1960–1975.

The closing prayer is from *A Cry for Mercy* (1981).

CHAPTER EIGHT: WHERE DO I BELONG?

Core material in this chapter is adapted from "Moving from Solitude to Community and Ministry" in *Leadership* (Spring 1995).

Adaptations of three published interviews are incorporated into this chapter: "How I Found My Way Home" is from "Faces of Faith," an interview with Arthur Boers, *The Other Side* (September–October 1989); "Life Together in Community" is adapted from Todd Brennan's article and interview "A Visit with Henri Nouwen," *The Critic* (Summer 1978); the story of Henri's emotional breakdown is from "Parting Words: A Conversation with Henri Nouwen," an interview with Rebecca Laird, *Sacred Journey* (September 1996).

Additional material is incorporated from "Some Reflections on Priestly Formation" (unpublished manuscript, ca 1987), *Bread for the Journey* (1997), *The Return of the Prodigal Son* (1992), *Finding My Way Home* (2001), and two journal entries (September 9 and the epilogue) from *Road to Daybreak* (1988).

"Suggestions for Community-Building" is adapted from Henri's "Some Suggestions for the Small Groups" developed as a handout for his spiritual formation class at Harvard (1984).

CHAPTER NINE: HOW CAN I BE OF SERVICE?

This chapter is an edited version of "Moving from Solitude to Community and Ministry," *Leadership* (Spring 1995) combined with "Parting Words: A Conversation with Henri Nouwen," an interview with Rebecca Laird, *Sacred Journey* (September 1996).

The story of Bill's spontaneous humor is from the unpublished transcript of a lecture "An Evening with Henri Nouwen" (St. James Church, New York, 1993) and from *In the Name of Jesus: Reflections on Christian Leadership* (1989).

"Gratitude and Compassion" is adapted from "Parting Words" and "Care and Ministry."

"Downward Mobility and Voluntary Displacement" is adapted from "Disappearing from the World," first published in *Sign* (1976).

Nouwen's reflection on the three promises he made on his thirtieth anniversary of ordination to the priesthood is excerpted from the epilogue to

The Road to Daybreak (1988). Additional excerpts are adapted from *The Wounded Healer* (1972), *With Burning Hearts* (1994), *Bread for the Journey* (1997), *The Road to Daybreak* (1988), and *Letters to Marc About Jesus* (1988).

EPILOGUE: WHERE DO I GO FROM HERE?
"The Parable of the Trapeze Artists" and the reflection on it are from *Our Greatest Gift* (1994).

Primary sources for Henri's emerging spirituality of the body include: "Our Story, Our Wisdom," in Robert Perelli, and Toni Lynn Gallagher, eds., *HIV/AIDS: The Second Decade* (1995). This article is a transcript of an address presented by Henri at Loyola University July 26, 1994.; *Our Greatest Gift: A Meditation on Dying and Caring* (1994); his unpublished personal notes on AIDS (1990); the December 28, January 24, March 6, May 19 and 20, and July 9 journal entries in *Sabbatical Journey: The Final Year* (1997); and "Bring Your Body Home," in *The Inner Voice of Love: A Journey Through Anguish to Freedom* (1996).

PERMISSIONS